Charles Foran

SKETCHES IN WINTER

A BEIJING POSTSCRIPT

Charles Foran (signature)

A Saturday Night Book

HarperCollins*PublishersLtd*

First Edition

Canadian Cataloguing in Publication Data

Foran, Charles, 1960-
    Sketches in winter

"A Saturday night book".
ISBN 0-00-215778-0

1. China — Social life and customs — 1976- . 2. China — History Tiananmen Square incident, 1989. 3. Students — China — Political activity. I. Title.

DS779.23.F6 1992   951.05′8   C92-093369-6

92 93 94 95 96 ❖ RRD 5 4 3 2 1

For my parents

In handbooks on Chinese traditional painting, an advice commonly given to the artist who wishes to learn to paint trees is to sketch them in winter, for then, without the seductive yet confused and blurry effect of their leafy masses, through their stark nudity they can best reveal their inner structure and specific character.

—Simon Leys

CONTENTS

ACKNOWLEDGMENTS

I am grateful to John Fraser, Iris Skeoch, Jan Whitford, Hugh Wilson and, most especially, David Manicom for their support and assistance. Mary Ladky made this book, and so much else, possible.

NOTES

The Chinese unit of currency is called the *yuan*, currently valued at approximately five to the Canadian dollar. The currency is issued in two forms: *renminbi*, for use by Chinese people, and Foreign Exchange Certificates (FEC), designed for foreigners inside the country. Smaller units include *jiao* and *fen*.

For the most part *Sketches in Winter* uses the *pinyin* romanization of the Chinese language. Thus, Canton is referred to as Guangzhou and Mao Tse-tung becomes Mao Zedong. The *pinyin* system pronounces most letters and words as they look, with certain key exceptions.

This book also boasts a large cast of characters. Chinese people are known by their family name first. Friends are free to address each other by the complete name, the given name or, especially among men, the surname only.

FOREWORD

No outsider ever emerges from China indifferent to the country or its people: not the longtime sojourner, not even the ten-day package trip tourist. Both the immediate and the deeply rooted contrasts with our own society are part of the reason for this phenomenon. So also are the mind-numbing statistics: the crowded panorama of daily life, which can leave you thinking you're on another planet; the inexplicable contradictions in Chinese society; and especially the vast, racially centric flow of history that stretches uninterrupted to our own time from the first mythic glimmerings of civilized sensibility.

The statistics are simply surreal. I remember once trying to accommodate what, on the surface, seemed a generous concession by Chairman Mao Zedong. The overwhelming majority of the billion Chinese people, said the "Great Helmsman" a few years before he died, were loyal and dutiful citizens. Even though not everyone was a member of the Chinese Communist Party, nevertheless ninety-five percent of the population appreciated what the Party had done to end imperialist degradations against China and supported the Party's main goals. Almost as an afterthought, Mao squared the equation by saying that only five percent of the population should be considered "bad elements." *Only five percent!* That's fifty million people, twice the population of Canada, and the principal justification for a whole network of cruel "labor-reform" prison camps, which remain a central emblem of Communist rule. Buried deep inside that afterthought are all the Chinese citizens who ever dared to differ substantially from the Party's rule and declined to recant. The statistic comes straight from hell.

Then there's the question of the remaining ninety-five percent in the larger prison camp. Taking even the most casual walk in any of China's great cities, or lesser cities, or towns, or villages, an outsider is constantly aware of what can seem a suffocating plenitude of humanity. There were times when I lived in China, at the end of the seventies, that strolling down Wang Fu Jing in Beijing, or along The Bund in Shanghai, left me with the queasy feeling I too was being drawn along helplessly inside Chairman Mao's huge fishing net. It wasn't a pleasant feeling, but it *was* a moment of communion with the Chinese people. In my time, any such moment was something to be savored because even such peripheral encounters with reality were so unusual.

The heavy burden of totalitarianism that Chairman Mao bequeathed the long-suffering Chinese people comes with all the usual side effects. Courage and cowardice march side by side through the story of Communist rule in China. So also do emancipation and victimization. In the late seventies, a full decade before Charles Foran went hopefully off to teach in the Middle Kingdom, you could spot the walking wounded on any city street. They were young and old. They shuffled along the busy sidewalks with their heads down, plodding ahead with only one tangible goal in life left to them—mere survival.

And yet, at the same time, there was also an extraordinary miracle of the human spirit unfolding. Men and women who, in their youthful fervor and initial naivete had bought the whole Maoist bag of tricks during the Cultural Revolution, began to struggle using their wits and humanity to overcome one of the most pervasive and repressive systems of control the world has ever known. Cajoled, tricked and jerked around in vicious ideological warfare, even those loyal to what they thought they understood about Maoism were ultimately all betrayed. The young were dispatched in their millions from urban centers to the countryside where they were simply forgotten, but forgotten in a distinctively Chinese way because their dreams—or what was left of their dreams—were effectively hemmed in by masters of red tape. Fighting all this, they clawed their way back by embracing common sense and common decency—the two concepts most dreaded by the Communists. The early stirring I witnessed in the late seventies at the Xidan Democracy Wall exploded in Charles Foran's time with the extraordinary, and then tragic, events of 1989 in Tiananmen Square.

In the West over the years, we have done many bad turns to the Chinese people. Vulnerable ourselves to the Communists' propaganda because of the more outrageous manifestations of an imperialist past, we swayed regularly between periods of intense curiosity and goodwill and those of massive indifference imbued with a special kind of contempt that held that *they* are different from *us*. Particularly during the Cultural Revolution, we licenced high academics and privileged writers—unthinking, unprincipled hacks every one of them—to be our middlemen and dictate our understanding. I still remember, a good year into my newspaper posting in Beijing, the shock of placing all my externally learned certitude up against individual Chinese people's experience. I never felt so naked in my life as story after story started spilling out and I had to face the reality that these people were remarkably like myself. It was a terrible moment: instead of being able to dismiss every seemingly bizarre or inexplicable or pathetic manifestation of Chinese behavior as something connected to a radically different culture, I was forced to consider how I and my friends and family would cope, given the same fate. And within this much narrower horizon, I had to redefine and broaden concepts of loyalty, courage and endurance.

Being connected, as E. M. Forster has famously pointed out, helps people transcend most of the claptrap associated with cultural differences or taboos. Of course Chinese history and culture are different from our own, but how on earth did it come to pass that this diversity in the human condition was used for so long to deny the condition itself to a quarter of the world's population? The antidote to statistical nightmares and the oppression of crowded streets is individual experience: individuals experiencing individuals, individuals reaching out to individuals. This is a complicated, often frustrating, and sometimes messy business, but it *is* the antidote.

The book you are about to read is extraordinary for many reasons—its style is luminous, its insights are trenchant and its varied forays into individual Chinese psyches are even pioneering—but none of them is as important as the singular fact that Charles Foran considers the cast of characters he here serves up as his brothers and sisters. As scholar and author Simon Leys says, "We are all Chinese." Once that breakthrough in thinking has been made, and you will see how dramatic a breakthrough it is in *Sketches in Winter*, no Chinese statistic, no Maoist threat, no "Yellow Peril" theory, no racial bugbear will ever frighten you by day or in the dark of night.

John Fraser
Toronto,
December, 1991

PROLOGUE

On June 7, 1989, my wife, Mary, and I were asked to leave the Beijing institute where we had taught since the previous September. The request was not unexpected. The massacre on Tiananmen Square four days before had shut the college down completely, depriving the faculty of both students to instruct (most undergraduates had abandoned the campus) and a compelling reason to stray outdoors (rumors suggested an impending civil war between rival army units who disagreed over the government's bloody tactics). Given the circumstances, and faced with the prospect of a foreigner's becoming involved in the uprising, possibly even getting killed, the school administration exercised its privilege—based on its ownership of most of our return tickets—to dismiss the international staff. Options were limited: to fly directly back to North America, to make the same trip via Hong Kong, or to arrange a one-way ticket to a less volatile city in the south. Eighteen hours after making a decision, we were skirting the phalanx of reporters who lingered outside the arrivals gate at Hong Kong airport, aghast at the idea of going on camera to explain why we had exercised our privilege as Westerners to flee China.

Once I was home, my impulse was to rage against the men who had perpetrated the massacre. These were venal individuals, bedecked in the red bunting of socialism to ensure their control over institutions designed to maintain totalitarian governance. Inflated by the slavish People's Liberation Army and the sycophantic Chinese Communist Party, they lorded over the country with a lethal combination of ineptness and disdain. Criticizing the Beijing gerontocracy made sense; it also felt good.

But there were complications. I had never met paramount leader Deng Xiaoping. Prime Minister Li Peng was a stranger to me, and Mao Zedong had died when I was sixteen years old. During our initial teaching stint, I knew only a certain group of academics at a certain college in a certain district of the capital. Acquaintances extended to a few cleaning and security people, one or two support staff and the odd businessman who resided on campus—no farmers, no factory workers, no mandarins. Our colleagues were mostly under the age of thirty-five, and in my case the majority were men. The group made a feeble cross-section and offered scant insight into the minds of the nine hundred million Chinese who resided outside the major cities.

Equally troubling was the enigma of the student movement. Unable to explain its startling rise—without warning, like a chick from an unincubated egg—I fared even less well at producing a coherent interpretation of events. The movement was an expression of collective will, or the agenda of a few insurrectionists; the galvanization of the national character, or a Western media-fed aberration; the refutation of a destructive mind-set, or a nihilistic flirtation with death; a break with history, or the continuation of an apparently eternal cycle of violence and oppression. The suggestion of intricacy, and often ambiguity, in these conjectures was disquieting. Analysis of any kind seemed almost an insult to the students, an undermining of their fervent optimism and youthful ideals. More important, analysis felt inadequate; to explain the movement, I needed first to explain the world its participants inhabited, what made things so dire, so constricting.

Consequently, in February 1990 we returned to the same teaching jobs at the same Beijing institute. Though martial law had been lifted

2

three months before, the city was still occupied by a conquering army and still haunted by specters. Daylight business was furtive, and at night the streets emptied. Officially, "the Turmoil," as the government had designated the demonstrations, had been cataloged and shelved, and with stability restored, foreign tourists due back to replenish coffers and the Asian Games forthcoming in September, all was well. Former party secretary Zhao Ziyang, loser in the leadership skirmish, was under house arrest, replaced by Shanghai cadre Jiang Zemin, a nonentity to most people. Deng Xiaoping ruled from retirement; Li Peng acted as henchman. The trials of Tiananmen activists were still nearly a year away, meaning the principals of the movement were either exiles, guests of the American embassy or else missing—probably in prison, possibly dead. Of the twenty-one "most wanted" dissidents, less than a dozen were accounted for, and most information turned out to be rumor.

When fugitive leader Zhai Weimin emerged in early March to tell journalists that a new democracy group had been formed in Beijing, the news should have reverberated across the city. But the twenty-three-year-old spoke only to foreigners, only briefly, and provided no evidence to support his astonishing contention. Besides, Beijingers were convinced the situation was hopeless; it wasn't the right time to act; Zhai Weimin and his cohorts didn't stand a chance. (Zhai was arrested that May trying to escape into the Soviet Union.) It was time to wait, to gossip, to lament all that had befallen ordinary folk who didn't know any more what was right or who was to blame. Winter seemed eternal, and yet spring would bring no relief. With April would come the first of the anniversaries, growing in significance as the date of June 4, 1990, loomed.

Most of the teachers and students we had known before the crackdown were still at the school. Though many appeared to be in flux— they were revising plans, devising escapes—in truth, these people were exactly where they had been a year before, and likely would be a year hence. That the stasis was the result of a vicious government and material poverty was undeniable. That these factors failed to fully account for the condition was, however, equally apparent, and begged further exploration.

China, perhaps more than any other country, distracts attention from the terrible lives of its citizens by presenting a tidy cultural hierarchy. Here, a birth is recorded as an abstraction: Peasant, Proletariat, Intellectual, Cadre. The West also enjoys labeling the Chinese: they are Mysterious, Inscrutable, Ancient, Long-Suffering. The country itself is Complex, Inward, Different, Singular. To be born an Intellectual of Reactionary parents, raised a Petit Bourgeois in an Inward culture perceived by outsiders as Mysterious is tantamount to being crowned an Untouchable, a concept rather than a human being. While in Beijing, I never met an intellectual of reactionary lineage and I never met anyone who was inscrutable.

Nor did I encounter a single Marxist-Leninist or market economy socialist or closet capitalist with democratic leanings. Individuals blurred categories, undermined abstractions. Always, though, they evinced an allegiance to a belief system of such ferocity it made the other labels seem superficial. The allegiance was often unconscious and occasionally reluctant. Likewise, the system itself was curiously impervious to definition. But it was there nonetheless, a muddy batch of racial myth, cultural creed and propaganda. Because they were at a university, our colleagues tended to be reflective about themselves and the society that had defined them so indelibly. Because the university was in Beijing, they were also exposed in small but regular doses to strains of alternative belief systems, alternative realities. The result was a community where messages were mixed and loyalties had become increasingly divided. As foreign teachers, we lived on the periphery of this community. Our window onto it was narrow and inset. Still, the glass was clear and the view the window afforded could be surprisingly expansive—perhaps not such a bad cross-section, after all.

The travels that carried my wife and me back to China were, of course, illusory. I may be free to wander the globe, but my thoughts remain hampered by ignorance and inclination. These failings are likely in evidence in the following pages, and I no doubt misjudge and mistake, coarsen where I should refine. Though the first six months of 1990 were hardly a happy time in the capital, I alone am responsible for the darkness that shades the narrative. Just as characters are both disguised and distilled, so are events and observations amplified. To amplify an account of the student movement, for example, I surround it with sketches of a more somber period, a decision meant not to demean but to contrast and contextualize. Similarily, to censor my own responses to happenings, especially if those responses are revealing, would serve to uphold the lie of the coolly detached "observer." In Beijing I was not detached, and frequently not cool.

I was also with some of the nicest people I have ever met, people whose quirks were familiar to me, much like my own; people who treated outsiders with courtesy and warmth; people I was delighted to share a meal with and am happy to call friends.

PART I

MEET ME IN ATLANTIC CITY

1

GUO YIDONG

I met Guo Yidong our first morning back at school. It was 6:00 A.M., a busy time on campus, and I had abandoned a fitful rest to join the faithful in their observances: *chi gong* and *tai chi*, badminton and basketball, aerobics, jogging, the lesser rigors of the power-walk. Though pathways were bustling, the majority of the congregation had flocked to the track. An oval within a circle, the four-hundred-meter loop offered the community its only acceptable course. Jogging off-campus was unthinkable. No student ventured into the surrounding streets for any but the most practical of reasons. To pass through the gates to the outside, to stray, was considered an incendiary act, as evidenced by the guards who noted, on days of political import, the names of those who entered or exited. Besides, the college was stuck in a barbarous neighborhood miles from the downtown, choked with dust and flies, the air smacking of night soil from nearby fields. The main roads were chaotic, a free-for-all of spewing buses, belching trucks, vans and cars veering into oncoming traffic, horse-drawn carts lumbering across lanes, pedicabs and bicycles, skittish pedestrians, not to mention the ubiquitous free-markets—cages of chickens, boxes of cigarettes, soda bottles atop blocks of ice—that clung to sloping street shoulders or nestled along the banks of fetid streams.

It was better inside. But even on campus the territory was divided. Lanes were the domain of vehicles. Paths belonged to badminton. Courts were for basketball, and selected patches of ground hosted soccer. Otherwise, all sports, leisure and social activities gravitated toward the track and the field within it. Laps were the thing at our institute. Going around and around was what everyone did.

Bundled in an overcoat, scarf and gloves, ignoring the vision-deadening hues of a February sunrise, I launched into an inside lane dominated by gossiping cafeteria staff and old ladies in wool hats. Students in cheap tracksuits trundled past, shivering like naked branches. An aerobics class, undaunted by the breeze, contorted atop a bunker-turned-dance-floor that divided the two bleachers east of the track, separated from the field by a row of trees planted in stark ignorance of the fundamental premise of spectator sports. Disco music thumped the air, all bass.

I was puffing along, smiling at smiles, returning hellos, when I recognized the distinctive shuffle—pigeon-toed, hands clasped behind the back—of Guo Yidong. I called to him and, catching up, watched Guo stop, draw to within fifteen centimeters of me and squint so intensely his entire face screwed up.

"I had heard you were returning," he said calmly. "I did not know it would be so soon."

"We arrived last night."

"Is Mary sleeping?"

I nodded. When Guo looked puzzled, I answered out loud, realizing what was wrong.

"Are you wearing contact lenses?" I said stupidly.

"Contact what?"

"Lenses. Instead of glasses."

He asked for a spelling, and definition, of the words. Guo was an English teacher, though around campus he was referred to as "the philosopher," in mocking admiration of his passion for philosophy and theology. He was also nearly blind, and had, since I'd known him, worn glasses so thick that his eyeballs appeared to float freely behind the lenses. The octagonal rims had drawn a line across a face that was relentlessly round: round chin, round cheeks, round smile. Rimless, Guo now resembled a full moon with a mustache and the filaments of a goatee.

Prescription glasses cost two months' wages. Had his been lost? Stolen?

"According to Taoism," Guo explained, "the mind should master the body. Eyes therefore can be strengthened through, ahem, metaphysical exercise. Wearing glasses only weakens the resolve needed to overcome what is merely a physical illusion."

"Can you see all right?"

"Not really."

"Aah," I said sagely.

"But it is too early to tell. It could take some time for the *chi* to begin to circulate freely, thereby regulating the body's weaknesses."

"Are you able to read?"

"Only with the book pressed, could I say, to my nose."

"What about television?"

"I listen to the dialogue."

Our philosophical pace was encumbering those joggers and power-walkers, often octogenarians beating their arms to simulate flight, directly behind us. Guo and I retreated onto the lip of the field, which was hard as asphalt and slick with frost. He wore blue sweatpants, black shoes, thin gloves and a green army jacket: the same clothes as last winter. Guo was the son of an Anhui province farmer and was terribly poor. He used the pause to formally welcome Mary and me back to the college, the city, the country, and to extend an open invitation to drink tea in his room. That accomplished, we resumed our conversation. I asked how he was feeling.

"I am suffering from *yin* these days," he replied. "My system has slowed. I am quiet, full of introspection. I would say that I have been in this condition since last summer."

"Were you *yang* before?"

"Possibly for a few weeks, during the student movement and the Turmoil. It was even more uncomfortable being *yang*. To be perpetually excited and active is not, ahem, to my taste."

"I think I may be perpetually *yang*," I offered.

"To us, many Westerners seem in a condition of high energy and restlessness. To you, we must appear quite passive and even, could I say, as a slug?"

"Sluggish."

Guo hiccuped—half humph, half laugh—at the word.

"Before the student movement," I said, "had you achieved a balance?"

"I was in good health, yes. According to traditional medicine, good health reflects balance, the smooth flow of *chi*. This is perhaps why I have suffered many colds and flus in recent months. Fortunately, none of my internal organs have been affected." Guo sniffled and dabbed at his nose with a gray handkerchief. "At the moment," he continued, "the imbalance is strictly external, not serious. It is acute rather than chronic."

We rounded a curve to start a new lap. Guo mentioned that he had begun taking walks every two to three hours, up to six daily, to stimulate his sclerotic system and stave off stasis. On sunny afternoons he ventured through the west gate to stroll in the neighborhood; otherwise, he too confined his activities to the campus—along the pathways, around the track.

Toward the center of the field was a scrum of pensioners engaged in sport. The athletes, including two women, were dressed in caps and running shoes, blue Mao suits puffed with underlying layers of wool. The sport consisted of launching a lemon disk through the air in the direction of the next point on a square. Though execution was erratic—the disk wobbled like a wounded bird—the participants howled in glee, praising even the feeblest airborne success. I gaped at this aberration. Guo also squinted.

"*Fei die*," he said. "Maybe, let me see, 'flying-plate'? It is the fashion these days. Do you play?"

"We call it Frisbee."

He requested an etymology. I couldn't provide one.

"Strange word," Guo commented.

"Funny game."

"Good for the circulation, perhaps," he said, bending to collect the flying-plate that had rolled to his feet. Guo found a grip, took aim and flung the disk. His toss was a thing of beauty: hard, level, cresting at the precise moment outstretched hands should have reined it in. The problem was marksmanship. The players stood northwest of us; Guo's shot was directed, and veered, northeast. I caught up with the *fei die* and charted a new course into a gusting wind. My toss went up, then down, surfed the surface, expired. An old man retrieved the Frisbee and waved his thanks.

I had a question for Guo. "What happened to your transfer to the medical college?" I said. "Are you still awaiting final clearance?"

Guo Yidong had applied to teach English at a college of traditional medicine, where he could also have fulfilled a lifelong ambition and doubled as a student. The transfer had been approved a few weeks before June 4.

"I wanted to discuss this with you," he said, fanning into a smile. "The transfer was canceled in July because of the, ahem, political situation."

"What did the transfer have to do with the political situation?"

"Nothing, of course. It was a personal matter. But according to conventional thinking, our institute would have lost face because I asked to leave, and also risked being accused of trying to rid themselves of a bad element." He hiccuped at the jargon, mawkish even in a foreign language. "Meanwhile, the other college would, according to the same conventional thinking, also have lost face because it accepted me, a person who might be, let me see, a ruffian or perhaps a counter-revolutionary." Guo frowned. "Something like that," he said with a shrug. "The result, in both cases, was paralysis. Quite typical, I would say, even normal, to be expected."

"I'm sorry."

"There is no need. Things are okay here. I have food, accommodation, a job. To ask for more is vanity. Last year I was vain."

"Because of excess *yang*?"

"Possibly," he agreed. "But also because of something you said in class that influenced my thinking."

Guo had audited a seminar in English literature that I gave during the winter of 1988–89. "What did I say?" I asked.

"A philosophical point. We were discussing modern philosophy, and you explained that some thinkers believed 'action is its own meaning.' We are the sum of our actions, nothing else. This idea was very new and exciting to me. Because of it, I decided to take control of the externals of my, ahem, life and transfer to the medical college."

"It was just an idea, Guo," I said, shaken.

"Naturally," he answered, touching my arm in reassurance. "Just a, could I say, abstraction. A delusion, maybe. But greatly appealing to me. *Action is its own meaning*," Guo concluded. "Quite dangerous, perhaps."

The cold had numbed my brain. The sports ground was emptying into the cafeterias, where breakfasts of rice gruel and steamed buns were being served up. The flying-plate contingent was gone, aerobics had ended, and only a few joggers remained. In the absence of voices, the wind rose to a whistle, the way it does in a desert. Full morning light was imminent. Yet the sky seemed darker, heavier, than an hour earlier. It started to rain.

"Was it so wrong to want to study medicine?" I asked.

"Not wrong," Guo replied, hands still clasped behind his back. "Just irrelevant. Whether I teach language or study medicine doesn't matter. Both are externals, and therefore illusory. Taoism stresses absorption in the inner self, to the extent that whatever occurs on the outside is, let me see, of no importance. I live in a prison but am free. I live in a palace but am a prisoner."

"Escapism?" I said, referring to an old argument.

"Escapism from what?"

"Are you really free?" I asked.

"Only when indifferent to freedom," he answered.

I laughed. "I apologize for leading you astray last spring," I said.

"I must have *wanted* to go astray. My ambition was my jailer. I blame no one but myself."

"It's raining," I observed, wiping rain from my brow.

"I believe so."

"We should get inside."

"Perhaps I will walk one more lap," Guo said.

We exchanged icy handshakes.

"Could I ask?" he said.

"Sure."

"Many of us were surprised ..."

"I'm not sure why," I began. "Mary and I were both disturbed by what happened ..." Then, glancing at his patient, avuncular face, I confessed a secret I had planned to guard closely. "I'm looking for a shape."

"A shape?"

"To all this ..." I said, gesturing. "It's an unhealthy obsession."

"Aah," Guo smiled. "Desire."

I ran back to the dormitory.

Our apartment was a palace. Though nominally only a three-room suite, the pea-green carpeting, velour furniture, stand-up closets and Lego cabinets, cockeyed chandeliers, refrigerator and stove, beeping telephone and twenty-one-inch color television made the flat a fantasy, an emblem, an affront. Hot water surged from taps early mornings and evenings. Heat coursed through groaning pipes at inexplicable hours of the day. Maids hammered on doors to change bedding or slosh down floors with buckets of dirty water. A phone call brought staff scurrying up the stairs to fix blinking lamps or unclog blocked plumbing arteries. Downstairs, behind the foyer, was an exclusive cafeteria where we dined in comfort and privacy. The head chef was the school banqueter, fabled for his sea cucumbers and pepper chicken.

Our apartment, identical in the smallest detail to every other foreign teacher's apartment in the foreign-teachers-only building, was constructed entirely of concrete: ceilings, floors, front and rear balconies, kitchen counter. It was an elevated bunker. Sounds did not pass between walls. Stairwells and hallways, however, served as amplifiers; a corridor conversation three flights below reached our kitchen verbatim. A ventilation shaft in the bathroom had the same effect, except there it was unnerving, a bug planted in the most intimate of places. The absence of wood and plaster left us cold.

The building functioned. The function fulfilled an agenda, a need so urgent and chronic it precluded, or had forgotten, not merely frills but human idiosyncrasies—gaudy curtains, funny doorbells, footprints in freshly poured sidewalks. But our apartment did display ample evidence of human fallibility. Sweating pipes ran down the outsides of walls, often following the capillaries of widening cracks and peeling paper. Heating units rattled, faucets shuddered while emitting rust-red water, and the toilet howled in displeasure at off-hour duties. Dust crept in under ill-fitted doors and the wind scattered papers across rooms, bolted windows notwithstanding. Those same windows shed caulking chips regularly, and one blustery afternoon a pane of bedroom glass simply fell out, shattering on the ground below.

We spent most of our time in the living room, a chamber notable for the fact that, despite its regal dimensions, it had no bed and dresser, no kitchen table, no refrigerator. Students squeezed six into a dormitory cell, unmarried teachers sharing a closet with a colleague, even assistant professors with families, parents, in-laws, likely a pet bird or fish, all in only a room and a half, were astonished. Our living room, they declared, was exceptional. It was also tacky, stuffed with hideous furniture and drapes, hung with paperclips, that parachuted onto guests without provocation.

I had endured the previous night in the room. Heat, water and electricity were turned off after 11:00 P.M., even in the dead of winter. Wrapped in a blanket, I sat in a chair watching my breath dissipate and words swim in a book. I also listened. A campus of concrete in a neighborhood of asphalt could claim the acoustics of a cathedral. The shouts of men outside the north gate three hundred meters away were crystalline. A train steaming toward downtown rattled atop rails laid four kilometers south of the institute. But I wasn't listening for these noises. I was awaiting the tanks, like the last time, and anticipating the rattle of gunfire, like the last time. A thundering tank resembles nothing in the world except a thundering tank. Gunfire, in contrast, can pass for firecrackers or the backfire of a vehicle. Gunfire can fool a person, lull him to death.

In my jet-lag delirium, enfolded in fabric, ears stinging from the cold, I distinguished gunshots and heard the skirl of tanks gouging up the south road. I heard these eight-month-old sounds, sounds that had followed Mary and me to Hong Kong to commiserate over a massacre that the color of our skin, and perhaps our timidity, had kept us from witnessing firsthand but not from experiencing in the hollows of our stomachs, and then had pursued us back to Canada, where we lived as if permanently short of breath, nomadic, frazzled, unable to reconcile or resolve or even distinguish private tragedies—ours, our friends'— from the great public tragedy of Tiananmen, until finally, at wits' end, floundering in a Plateau apartment in a deep Montreal winter night, we received a phone call, an invitation from our former employer to make good on a promise, redress a betrayal, refocus images in danger of dissolving forever, and so we boarded a sequence of flights home to a city, a past, that held the key, we both sensed, to our ability to ever envision a future. Hearing those sounds again inside my head, a deep Beijing winter night all around, I felt beads of sweat, icy and sharp and not in the least like tears, race down my cheeks.

2

ZHOU SHUREN

"I cannot imagine my life without beer," Zhou said, emptying a second bottle. His pouring technique, the fruit of countless tipplings, was a thrill; the spout was inverted into the glass to pressure the liquid upward like a geyser, drowning the bottle neck in suds that surged to the rim and would have spilled over had Zhou not closed the sluice gates in the nick of time. The product, a masterpiece of form—effervescent wheaten body, foamy white head—lasted only a few seconds.

"Liquid courage," he added, draining the glass.

"Nice expression," I said.

"'Tequila Sunrise,' by The Eagles," Zhou explained. He sang, "'Welcome to the Hotel California.'"

"There are more bottles in the fridge."

"Good. Cold beer is much better."

"Do you want something to eat?" Mary asked.

"I ate six sparrows in Xidan Street this afternoon."

Mary groaned.

"I'm sorry, Mary," Zhou said. "I could not control myself. They were too delicious."

18

"You ate *six* sparrows?"

"I wanted to eat six more, but I had no money left. The flesh of baby birds is tender and sweet."

"How were they served?" I asked.

"On a stick."

"Six on one stick?"

"Like students in a dormitory room," he nodded.

Zhou Shuren was an artist as yet undiscovered by his art. He taught film in the English department, a job that consisted of knowing how to operate a video-recorder and supplying introductions to the American movies that were the highlight of the undergraduates' week, otherwise a tonal hum of grammar and vocabulary, listening skills, political studies. A native of Qinghai province in the northwest, Zhou was distinguished by his sunburnt skin and round Arab eyes that betrayed a hint of racial intermingling, always a scandal. He kept his hair long and oily, wore scruffy clothes and untied sneakers, sported a Walkman during staff meetings, smelled of hops and bad living and spoke a lilting English that often startled with its richness and depth. His passions were volatile—films, music, Westerners—and his "stance," a self-conscious nihilism that managed to both mock *and* embody the anguish of intellectuals, fingered him as a prime renegade. But for all that, Zhou remained at large, guarded by mentors in the department and by the insidious safety net of the university-as-work-unit, an ethos that led the institution to "protect its own" whenever possible, for reasons of politics and face, then ruthlessly purge the deviant from within, as a family matter.

He had got caught in the net last year. As friend of the artists who sculpted the "Goddess of Democracy" statue, Zhou had fled the campus the night after the crackdown and disappeared from Beijing. He was eventually arrested and incarcerated, but then suddenly reappeared at school and resumed, however erratically, his duties. Opinions on his resurrection were divided. For many of his students, especially the young women, Zhou was a dashing figure: a basically decent rebel, a deep-down patriotic iconoclast, just like in the movies. Others took a harder line and wished him no good. Zhou himself was unambiguous. "I am stupid," he told us. "The stupidest person in the world."

"Why?"

"Because I live here."

"Do you have a choice?"

"I am stupid, and everyone else is stupid also. We are all very, very stupid. But I am definitely the worst."

I opened a fresh bottle.

"Because I *know* I am stupid," he continued. "And I know that *they* are stupid, too. Knowing you are stupid when you can't ever be smart is very, very stupid. That makes me—"

"Do you like the music?" I interrupted.

Zhou's left leg was pumping to the beat. We had brought him gifts: The Rolling Stones, R.E.M., Talking Heads, compilations of 80s hits. Rock and roll was a Rubicon that Zhou Shuren alone cared to cross. Most friends were appalled by the music. It was too harsh and aggressive, rife with stridency about topics—sex, violence, politics—that made cheeks flush. Music that was not melodious was hardly music at all. Oddly, students were the most adamant in rejecting rock and roll. Babbling brooks, country villages, innocent love, home-as-the-heart—these were the clichés that undergraduates lived by, a cocoon of insouciance whose musical equivalent, both in lyrics and melody, was predictably banal. John Denver and The Carpenters vied with Taiwan ditties for supremacy. Denver's "Country Roads" was a paean to place, Karen Carpenter's "It's Yesterday Once More" a hymn to times gone by. Confronted with Prince or even the Paul Simon of *Graceland*, students winced and chattered nervously until their collective disapproval suffocated the menace. Functioning as a chorus was satisfying to most; the refutation emerged so naturally and with such resolve that it appeared rehearsed, a ritualized exercise in catharsis.

Not so with Zhou. Among his social networks outside the university was the entourage that surrounded the country's sole genuine rock musician, Cui Jian. Through this connection, and his numerous Western friends, Zhou had access to an FM playlist of current material, influences officially unwelcome in the People's Republic. Zhou welcomed any and all influences into his Walkman. His tastes were eclectic and inclusive, so far off the map it was easy to forget how miraculous such aesthetic openness was.

"It's okay," he answered, referring to a Van Morrison tape. "But maybe too slow."

"He's more of a soul singer," I said.

"I am a socialist," Zhou offered. "We have no souls." He inverted the bottle into his glass again. The foam rushed to the rim as before. Except that with this round, reflexes dulled, Zhou hesitated a split second; the spout emerged from the head chased by trickles of beer. "Sorry," he said, wiping the table with a finger.

"Are you sure you don't want something to eat?" Mary asked.

"I cannot imagine my life without beer," Zhou replied.

I was anxious to direct the conversation back to June. Letters to Canada from other friends had only reported Zhou's safety, avoiding details for fear of censors. Zhou had wisely kept mute. What had happened to him?

"I wanted to write to you," he said, forming a church steeple with his hands, "but it was impossible. I am—" he lowered his voice "—not yet clear of trouble."

"Do you think—?" I said.

"Maybe," he answered quickly.

Everyone speculated about listening devices in the apartments. One man, certain the bug was in the telephone, buried the instrument inside a desk whenever he had guests. Others preferred to meet students outdoors or in noisy cafeterias.

"Do you want to go somewhere?" I asked.

"It's okay. They know already."

I turned Van Morrison up a notch, just in case.

"I left Beijing after visiting you the night of June 5," he began. "A train to Chengdu, Sichuan province. Beijing station was full of soldiers but also thousands of people trying to escape. I had to buy a ticket on the black market for one hundred *yuan*."

"Why Chengdu?"

"It was the only ticket available. I didn't care where I went. Just away from here, you see, and the army. They were killing people in the streets around the station that night. I did not want to die." He stopped to order his thoughts. "At the time, I couldn't picture my life twenty-four hours into the future. Now I cannot picture my life eight months into the past. What have I been doing since then? Probably it wouldn't have mattered if a soldier had shot me in Beijing station. Stupid people are better off dead, don't you think?"

Zhou cast us a sidelong glance, tossing his head to clear hair from his eyes. We smiled weakly.

"Before leaving my room I put my Walkman and four cassettes into a bag," he said. "No food or clothes. Just U2, Sade, The Rolling Stones and a Duran Duran tape a French student gave me. For two days I sat on the train listening to rock and roll." Zhou paused to sing the chorus of U2's "Sunday, Bloody Sunday." Then he resumed. "The car was very crowded. People slept under seats, in between seats, on top of each other, some even up on the shelves where luggage is kept. At each stop, soldiers tried to board the car to look for fugitives, but they lacked the will to climb over bodies to the middle of the cabin, where I sat with a family of farmers from Shaanxi. The farmers were totally ignorant, you see, ignorant of politics, culture, geography, and so could enjoy themselves—eat seeds, play cards, spit out the window. Watching these people was educational. I like being among peasants.

"The family were kind. They shared their food with me. I also bought the awful food sold on platforms and read the stupid magazines that everyone reads. The farther south we went, the more crowded the train became. To use the toilet, I had to wake up the man who was living in there! But the trip was okay," he decided.

"Then you arrived in Chengdu?"

"That's right. The station was full of soldiers and the downtown streets were patrolled by tanks."

Though largely unreported, the rioting in Chengdu, in the wake of events in Beijing, had been bloody.

"Not the best city to escape to," I said.

"Very, very stupid," he agreed. "I was arrested on the platform by Public Security. Two days on the train, two nights in the jail. The police brought me to a room to ask questions about the student movement. They were positive I was an important leader. All my things were placed on a table, including a copy of *The Catcher in the Rye* in English. Very suspicious, they said. Must be Western propaganda."

We mulled that one over.

"But the officers were most interested in the cassettes. The Duran Duran tape was not prerecorded, so they decided that it must contain speeches made from Tiananmen Square. The police played the cassette twice and made me translate the lyrics. The song 'The Big Thing' was suspicious," Zhou said, smiling at the memory. "A line about not wanting a girl's love was provocative, and concealed a message telling citizens to reject the Party's rule. I translated from English and told the police that the song was probably about sex."

"What did they say?"

"They were extremely stupid, you see. My head pounded from listening to Duran Duran so many times. But do you know what was worst?"

"The police beat you?"

"I *hate* Duran Duran," Zhou said. "The cassette had no name on it, and I had taken it from my drawer by mistake. Because of this error I had to hear all the songs twice, in a room with sweating men who smoked cheap cigarettes. The police gave me tea, though, in a big jar that I shook every few minutes to observe the leaves swirl and settle."

"What about the sex?"

Zhou's smile spread as he refilled his glass. His hands, though, trembled slightly. "The men told their chief that I had sex on a cassette. As a result, I had to wait an extra day in a cell with twenty other criminals. I was interrogated by the chief. He made me translate the songs again! Then he got angry when he did not find enough sex. It was," Zhou concluded, pausing for effect, "torture."

"Then what happened?"

"I was released and put on a train to Xi'an. The police said they had enough problems with their own people to bother with a Beijing

counterrevolutionary. Besides, I wasn't a very interesting or important counterrevolutionary. I was disappointing."

"Did they keep Duran Duran?"

"I offered the cassette to them."

"No takers?"

"The police didn't like the music either."

"Happy ending," I said.

"That's right," Zhou said, relaxing in his chair. "During the first
interrogation I told the officers that I once won an award for compos-
ing a criticism of Liu Shaoqi. In my criticism, I exposed the ultra-
Rightism and reactionary agenda of the Liu Shaoqi clique, including
an explanation of how Liu put on an extreme-Left mask to disguise a
Right essence." Zhou gulped his beer. "The teacher claimed I had a
bright future and awarded me a Mao button that was visible in the
dark. Our class devoted a year to criticizing Liu Shaoqi. There was a
great deal of information on the subject. I composed a speech about
Liu in my head because I could not write. I did not know where
Canada was or who was the leader of the Soviet Union. I could not
add numbers or read more than a few basic characters. I was a revolutionary hero," he summarized. "I was six years old."

We waited.

"I wanted to confess to the police," Zhou said. "I was terrified, you
see, and feeling bad about my stupidity. I wanted to explain why I was
such a stupid person, and also why they were such stupid people, too."

"Did you tell the police they were stupid?"

My question was tactless. The bruises below Zhou's eyes and the
intensity of his nervous tics—the toss of the head, the darting
glances—were stark signs. He had fought despondency for an hour.
But now, drunk, his tale told, the will was waning. A desultory last beer
trick ended in disaster. Rivulets of liquid were moving across the table
before Zhou even thought to withdraw the spout. Cursing, he
knocked over the bottle and the glass, diverting more suds onto the
carpet with the sweep of a forearm intended as a mop.

"Down with Liu Shaoqi!" Zhou said, rising.

We stuffed his coat with cassettes.

"I'm glad you're back," he said, shaking my hand before embracing Mary. His eyes welled. At the door, he offered lines from Cui Jian:

"*Bu shi wu bu ming bai,*
Zhe shijie bian hua kuai."
("It's not that I don't understand,
The world just changes too fast.")

Zhou tripped negotiating the stairs between the third and second floors. We heard a thump, bad language, then an assurance that he was, he thought, he had to admit, he was resigned to the fact, okay (but still stupid).

Zhou Shuren, who had disappeared, was okay.

People disappeared all the time. A woman Mary knew last year arranged a visa for herself and her daughter, obtained passports, quit her job and sneaked off to Australia two weeks before our return, telling not a soul. Friends learned of her departure only when someone else—who was alloted her apartment as a favor, in return for a favor, to curry a favor for future use—answered her door. One department lost nineteen teachers in three years. They'd gone AWOL in America, Canada, Australia and England, leaving desks, rooms, teaching schedules; leaving unfinished theses, half-written books, bits of translations, outstanding debts; leaving fiancés, wives, husbands, children, parents, grandparents. A visa, be it for the purposes of scholar, student or even tourist, portended a vanishing. A visa meant a hypothetical loss that could not be mourned because no one would admit it had occurred. A visa meant rumors, innuendo, hastily called meetings to deny culpability, assign blame, and then to quietly up the body count by arranging the requisite banquets and gifts-left-on-tables to ensure the disappearances continued.

Everyone understood; no one forgave. Ill will rarely surfaced; resentment ate away at the guts. For every scholar who got out, a dozen who longed to stayed. Resources, connections, tenacity: some had them, others were lacking. Ambivalence kept things in check. Outside was marvelous, of course, but what about the decay and poverty and gangs of vicious blacks? Propaganda painted Bosch-like portraits of the outside. Inside, in contrast, was safe and warm, a guarantee of cups of tea and bowls of rice, regardless of prickliness or dissatisfaction or even, to a point, wayward tendencies.

I spent two sleepless nights listening for tanks and reading translations of the country's leading missing person, Wei Jingsheng. An electrician by trade, Wei had edited a magazine during a brief but pivotal Beijing democracy movement in 1978 that ended with the arrest and trail of key "scum of the nation," as the state prosecutor described the Democracy Wall reformers. Wei's essays, including an exposé of the notorious Qincheng prison north of Beijing, had made him the primary target. I was looking at the Qincheng article:

> Living conditions at Q1 [Qincheng] are enough in themselves to destroy an ordinary man's will. If one did not know that many of the inmates were among the finest people that China has produced, one could easily mistake the place for a lunatic asylum, or a penitentiary for prisoners sentenced to death ...
>
> The torments of daily life are not enough to break the will of these stalwart people. Q1 is therefore equipped with instruments which cause terrible pain in the head during interrogation. When the pain becomes unbearable, and the prisoner is writhing around on the ground, the pain suddenly ceases, only to resume again just as suddenly, and so on, until either a confession is extracted or the interrogators conclude that the techniques are proving ineffective.

Also the transcript of his famous trial defense:

> Dissent may not always be pleasant to listen to, and it is inevitable that it will sometimes be misguided. But it is everyone's sovereign right. Indeed, when government is seen as defective or unreasonable, criticizing it is an unshirkable duty. Only through the people's criticism and supervision of the leadership can mistakes be minimized and government prevented from riding roughshod over the masses. Then, and only then, can everyone breathe freely.

Wei Jingsheng was sentenced to fifteen years for counterrevolutionary activities. Photos of his October 1979 trial were circulated, but after that date he vanished. Cell 11, Block 2, Beijing prison #1 is where Wei was believed to have spent four years in solitary confinement, a status that permitted no visitors, no contact with fellow prisoners and only a single hour of outdoor exercise per month. The dissident engaged in hunger strikes and other contentious pastimes, for which he was duly punished. In 1984, amid reports of nervous breakdowns and bouts of schizophrenia, Wei was probably transferred to a labor camp in the northwest, where his condition was rumored to have further deteriorated. People said he went insane. People even whispered that he was dead. Officials refused to comment on their convict, verifying his existence only after the question was asked by a foreign politican. Wei was apparently still breathing.

An Australian translator I met claimed that his housekeeper once worked in Qincheng itself, where she had personally fed a Mr. Wei his daily rice gruel. The Wei Jingsheng the woman described was a shattered soul with screaming eyes and quivering lips. He never spoke, rarely ate, barely squirmed inside his cell. But the housekeeper, who changed jobs in the mid 1980s, was recalling a bygone era. Her memory was erratic. The year, the prisoner, the prison—how could she be certain of what she had witnessed? She didn't want trouble. Strangely, however, once a month the woman retold her Wei Jingsheng story to the Australian, launching into it brusquely, almost in shame, as if an ancient curse obliged her to keep repeating the same terrible tale.

3

DING LUOJIN

We invited one of Mary's favorite students to dinner in a restaurant our second weekend on campus. Ding Luojin was a twenty-one-year-old from Hunan who had gained entrance into the college by finishing first in her province in English. Now a senior, Luojin had witnessed too much and been too changed to contemplate returning to her hometown. But the Turmoil of 1989 had so shocked and sickened her that she could also no longer tolerate Beijing. She hated the school, the city, the country; she had to escape, to locate a place where everyone was not insane. Before the massacre, Luojin would have conjured mountain streams, frolicking wildlife, cantings of light across a cabin floor as her idyll; by March 1990, she wanted a secretarial job with a company in Shenzhen, a special economic zone that bordered Hong Kong. "If I have money," she explained to us on the way to the restaurant, her English soft and musical, "I can be my own person. I can be me. That is the only hope for someone living here."

"How will money let you be you?" Mary asked.

Luojin giggled, brushing hair from her eyes. Though tall and heavy, she was an elegant person, her physical manner and deliberate, thoughtful way of speaking mirroring a singular personality.

"I am not sure," she replied. "But perhaps money will allow me not to be so frightened of everything!" Luojin laughed again, then quickly sobered. "I just want to be left alone. Most students feel this way. Our lives belong to everyone but us. Money can buy peace, I think, and maybe freedom."

"What about letting you be you?"

"People are all strangers. To each other, and to themselves. It is quite horrible," she said evenly.

"Will you be able to choose your job after graduation?" I asked, knowing the answer.

"Of course not."

"Who assigns students their jobs?"

"The school. The department. Dean Shen, probably."

"Where do you think—?"

She cut me off. "I have no connections in Beijing. I will be sent back to my hometown, probably to work in a travel agency."

"Does your hometown get many tourists?"

"Never."

"Do people from your hometown travel abroad?"

"Almost never."

"How do you plan to get into Shenzhen?"

"I have an uncle ..." Luojin began.

Ding Luojin had an uncle whose second cousin had once worked for a Shenzhen company but was now retired back in the hometown. As a favor, this uncle would pay the second cousin a rare visit to present Luojin's case (a carton of Marlboro cigarettes) and solicit, in return for a favor contracted during a visit a decade before, his assistance in arranging both a passport (bottles of *mao tai* liquor) and a meeting with contacts (two hundred *yuan*) within his former company. Assuming the second cousin was amenable, Luojin would proceed to the border—special economic zones, especially Shenzhen, were sealed off from the rest of the country to hide their wealth—provisioned with the requisite letters of introduction (two more cartons of

Marlboros) and a sack of token gifts to remove token impediments. Once inside Shenzhen, she believed life would be bountiful: jobs a-begging, spacious apartments waiting with open doors, the ascendancy of commerce and the fairly free flow of capital cutting those capricious and counterproductive forces down to size (i.e., bureaucrats could always be bought off). Her future secured, Luojin need only skip back to her hometown and drop by her newly assigned work unit to make arrangements (cigarettes, liquor and cash) to be either stricken from the list of residents, thereby vanishing into the demographic mists, or else, more likely, to join the ranks of citizens who continued to officially labor, reside and, most important, be paid by a unit they had not gone near in years. (Salaries were diverted into the appropriate pockets.) Simple, Luojin concluded. A-B-C.

The restaurant was tucked behind a classroom building. Designed for the faculty, it boasted inflated prices, soiled tablecloths and decent food prepared by a local family. In 1988, the clientele had been almost exclusively staff, with student bohemians and blushing couples cowering in corners lest they be noticed, and chided for laziness, by their professors. During the two years intervening, however, the spending power of teachers had plummeted; those not busy seeking alternative employment were saving their meager salaries for payment toward international airline tickets. Students had also been transformed. The distinctly Western habit of borrowing cash from parents, until recently an offense to familial propriety, was now a respected, even fashionable practice. Likewise the part-time job, often of dubious legality, which generated income to be disposed of quickly, publicly, with fanfare and bravado.

Fireworks were certainly popping in the restaurant that evening. The room was a den of aspiring iniquity. Tables were jammed with tipsy students, mostly male, all flushed and overheated in their fake leather jackets and slim black ties. For these young men, speaking in a normal tone of voice smacked of scholarship; one had to shout, preferably while pounding the tabletop, chopsticks cutting the air and drinks sloshing over rims. A couple of dishes and a glass of beer per person reeked of intellectual conservatism; the table had to sag under the weight of fancy foods—chopped chickens, marine delicacies, fish fossils swimming in sauces—and dozens of seaweed-green bottles. Gourmands smoked cigarettes between bites, hawked lustily before spitting on the floor, swept animal bones off the table and, in pursuit of the crowning cliché of cadre bacchanal, shouted themselves hoarse playing a drinking game that involved guessing the number of fingers an opponent would raise, the loser being required to drain his glass as penalty. I recognized several of my own students among the epicureans, and Mary chatted with a couple of fire-breathing bucks whose pie-eyed glances were part smitten, part sodden, and whose English was suddenly as skeletal as the fish. Not surprisingly, the restaurant was devoid of educators.

"Wow," we both commented.

"There are seats over there," Luojin said.

I ordered from a ticket window under siege by a gang of soccer hooligans waving hundred-*yuan* bills and carrying on in the manner usually reserved for train stations and bus stops. The jostling was pure locker room, exuding displaced sexual energy and don't-give-a-fuck posturing. Actually, the undergraduates only affected a rebel stance; the group that was serving as their unconscious model was that of the Party and state cadres devouring public funds and toasting one another into alcoholic stupors at banquets. Beijing restaurants were chock-a-block with these ghastly demonstrations of corruption and waste. The students were behaving like the bureaucrats those with family and connections—the fabled *guanxi* of society—would likely become.

Luojin was apparently dismayed. "Students are acting badly these days," she said. "They have no respect for anything. Every night they eat and drink until they run out of money."

"Do they study?"

"No one studies. It is pointless. Our jobs have already been decided for us. What we do makes no difference."

"These students must have good job assignments," Mary said.

"Probably," Luojin agreed, pulling back her hair. "Many of them are the sons of important officials and businessmen. I think they will run the country soon. They are," she added, observing a boy lurch into a table, "very ugly."

"We could eat someplace else," I said.

"Where?"

"The restaurant outside the north gate is okay."

"It is dirty," she mentioned.

"A little."

"And the people who eat there are common. Mostly farmers and construction workers from the countryside. I cannot understand their dialects. Those men are crude and uneducated."

"You don't like eating off campus?"

"Peasants are different from us," Luojin explained. "We do not feel much closeness to them. Peasants care nothing for education or culture or international affairs. We are uncomfortable in the restaurants around the campus. It is better in here."

"Who's 'we'?" I asked.

"Intellectuals."

A conference of intellectuals at the next table was debating with passion the theorem by which the sum of five might be obtained using those appendages affixed to the right hand. One scholar, despairing of ever breaking the code, hoisted a commiserative beverage and downed it, mostly onto his shirt. Fellow sages expressed their sympathy through colorful gestures and expressions.

"Terrible!" Luojin said, unable to conceal her affection for the merrymakers. "They are so drunk!"

Dinner arrived. Luojin assessed the meal like a testy critic; dishes were sniffed, sauces tasted, color and texture commented on until, finally, a miserly bite was chewed. During the lengthy pauses in between, chopsticks pressed meditatively to her lips, she would eye the plates critically, daring a failed concoction to remain in her sight. Opinions, however, were kept private. Only after a full half hour of bird-feeding did Luojin's eyes suddenly widen as, aesthetic duty done, she tucked into the now cold food, sparing no leftovers. Two bowls of rice were also consumed.

"The rice is good," she said out of the blue. "Though maybe too dry."

Dinner was over.

We maneuvered around various disaster areas to the exit, ignoring the smeared tablecloths and bones that crunched beneath our feet. The air outside was bitter. I had a question for Luojin.

"Do *you* study?" I said. She was, after all, my student now.

"Rarely," she answered. "But I like to listen to your lectures."

"Because of my accent?"

"Students like the American accent," she confirmed. "We all want to copy it."

"What about what I say?"

Luojin giggled. Mary bailed her out. "How do you spend your time if you don't study?" she asked.

"I read in my dormitory room."

"What are you reading?"

"*Gone with the Wind.*"

"In English?"

She giggled some more. Students in depair sought the solace of translations. English was too painful, too emblematic, to endure during troubled times. At the beginning of the term I asked my senior class to list the books they had read between September and February. Though all the students claimed to read in English, the titles they came up with were odd. Hemingway was the favorite: *The Old Man and His Fish* and *Goodbye, Arm.* One young man insisted he had devoured the five hundred pages of John Steinbeck's masterpiece in the original. Which Steinbeck masterpiece? *The Angry Grapes,* the student claimed proudly.

"Sometimes I read in English," Luojin said. "But it is too hard and slow. I want to get through the story fast, like a movie. Mr. Zhou showed us the movie of *Gone with the Wind* in November."

"Could you understand the accents?"

"There were words on the screen."

"Words?"

"Characters, actually ... at the bottom ..."

"Subtitles," I said.

"Yes."

"*Gone with the Wind* is a long novel," Mary offered.

"We choose only long novels," Luojin said. "The more pages in the book, the more hours it takes to read. That way we can spend all day in bed."

"What else do you read?"

"Nothing else. Only long novels."

"Who's 'we'?" I repeated.

"My roommates. Many days we stay in our dormitory and read. It is better than going outside."

"Outside the campus?"

"Outside the room."

"All six of you, all day?"

"We forget together," Luojin explained.

Neither of us asked.

We reached her dormitory. A naked bulb above the door cast a feeble arc over the ground, enough light, apparently, for the two women on the sidewalk enjoying the latest sporting fad. The students squeaked in their winter coats and squealed with each toss.

"Do you play flying-plate?" I asked Luojin.

"Frisbee, silly!" she corrected.

For provincial students like Ding Luojin, a first in a subject was often the only way to guarantee themselves a spot at a Beijing university. Once they were accepted, considerations of subject matter and funding vanished; the point was to be in the capital, the country's cultural and political omphalos. Though Shanghai was more dynamic and Guangzhou was faster paced, Beijing was where things happened.

In a famine-plagued society, a soccer-ball paunch boasted the red meat and bottomless rice bowl of prosperity. To call a person fat was a compliment, conferring respect and acknowledging supremacy on the basis of material might. In this sense, the principal symbols of authority in Beijing—the Forbidden City, the municipal offices, the Party leadership compound known as Zhongnanhai—were all rotund mandarins ensconced at dinner tables, boasting the bloated dimensions associated with dominance. The halls of power were never literally lofty, as in Athens or Lhasa. Other strategies were used to inculcate the idea of feudal hierarchy. First, the sprawling palaces were self-contained units that were expressly off-limits to the public. They had apparently plummeted from heaven, squat Olympuses in the heart of an urban landscape to which they were in no way connected. "Pekingers" had walked, bicycled or rickshawed around the Forbidden City in 1890 as if it were a square mile of moonrock, which, in effect, it was. Modern Beijingers walked, bicycled and drove cars around Zhongnanhai with similar attitudes. If execution for sneaking into either of these fortresses wasn't sufficient deterrent to the curious, the bewilderment occasioned by attempting to penetrate their defenses would be. Once within the gate, the intruder would encounter a stultifying array of pavilions, halls and temples, labyrinths of lanes and passages that advanced, or withdrew, into courtyards, cul-de-sacs, gardens, parks, hills and lakes. Doors would bolt gently behind the interloper; city sounds would dwindle and be replaced by the sounds of this city, this universe of countries within countries, governments within governments. All power and authority emanated from downtown Beijing while remaining utterly alien and indistinct. Who was really in charge? Miles of imperial-red walls made it impossible to tell.

In the mid-1980s, foreign firms began to alter the cityscape. Office towers and hotels of twenty, fifty and finally eighty floors were ordered and hastily constructed. Though the government muscled half ownership of these behemoths, their names alone betrayed the significant partner: New World Tower, World Trade Center, Beijing International Hotel, Great Wall–Sheraton Hotel. Vertical might, especially the glass columns that diverted sunlight and cast playful shadows across miles of urban sprawl, challenged the traditional order. The differences revolved around a single, potent association: no mere buildings, the towers embodied fabled and, until recently, decadent principles of international commerce and marketing, the exchange of technology, the drive toward modernization. Towers *were* the outside world, and in contemporary Beijing that was an exciting, alluring, ultimately dangerous idea.

Nineteen-year-olds arriving in the capital for the first time were shocked by the anomalies. Certain students, confident and daring, found in the city skyline confirmation of, even support for, their own developing sensibilities as iconoclasts. But for many provincial undergraduates, and certainly those who ended up at a middle-ranked institute like our own, the office towers were sources of unease. How, for example, could the owners of the massive World Trade Center on Jianguo men wai Street, unfinished at the time of the demonstrations and then sprayed with bullets by nervous soldiers in the days following the massacre, have blithely resumed construction in the summer and fall of 1989, and now be promoting its grand opening in the newspapers? Beijing was full of such imponderables, and the majority of students we taught, chastened by the crackdown and the apparent dangers of associative thinking, preferred not to grapple with them. Better to stay on campus and play *mah-jong*, organize skits and song contests, hold dance parties on Friday nights.

Mary and I dropped by the classroom building after walking Ding Luojin back to her dormitory. Younger students especially spent ten hours a day, seven days a week, in their classrooms. Assigned a class, and a room, the first day at college, undergraduates bonded with their classmates to the exclusion of colleagues a year above and below and often those only a wall apart, in the adjoining chamber. Class Three, composed of the brightest state scholarship kids (based on entrance exam scores), consorted regularly with Class One (also bright), irregularly with Class Two (so-so, but lively), never at all with Classes Four and Five (fair to middling), and refused to acknowledge the existence of Classes Six and Seven (students whose parents or work units had paid the tuition). The classroom served as study hall, gymnasium, dining facility, theater and party haven. Book-laden teachers shuffled from corridor to corridor; undergraduates stayed put class after class, semester after semester. The desk asssigned to a body in September 1986 was the desk occupied by that body in March 1990. Likewise for the deskmate and, in most cases, the dorm mate: same person, same position, same place.

Dance parties were sweet. The room was decorated—streamers, crepe paper over the lights, chalk drawings on the blackboard—and well supplied with bowls of apples and bottles of yellow soda. Desks were pushed against the walls to enlarge the floor; a tape-player perched atop the lecturer's podium. The evening commenced with speeches by the homeroom teacher, often a recent graduate, and the class monitor, a model student selected by the department. The speeches were, like all speeches delivered in public, formal, even ritualized, relying on stock phrases, rote expressions, mannerisms mimicked from elders. Next, the foreign guests were introduced, applauded and implored to sing a song later in the evening.

Finally the dancing started. It was a little like a scene from *Gone with the Wind*, with subtitles. Couples, often both female, waltzed in stiff pleasure to tapes of Strauss and classical Muzak. *One-two-three, one-two-three*, the steps had been memorized and rehearsed in anticipation of the event. Though waltzes were the rage—classes had been given on campus in 1988—repertoires also included the rhumba and fox trot, the racuous jitterbug. Undergraduates danced the way they spoke English. Decorum was all: posture, expression, movements carefully plotted and gracefully executed. Glitches were laughed at, unless committed by notorious clods (i.e., us). Mary had a full dance card and flourished. I was hopeless. While lurching over the concrete (*one-three-two*) with a nervous sophomore, I asked questions about the institute, Beijing, being away from home. Though polite, her answers were resolutely shallow. Those young women who dared engage me in conversation did so with eyes that were intelligent but also fearful, begging to be left alone. Students didn't really want to talk; students just wanted to dance.

Dean Shen joined the party. His outline in the doorway drew gasps, and within seconds of crossing the threshold the English department head had a soda in one hand, an apple in the other, and was rejecting offers of nuts. Shen Yanbing was a forty-five-year-old with disheveled hair and gray stubble on his cheeks. Though an established academic, he wore the look of a hunted man: pale, bleary-eyed, primed to explode at the strike of a match. The dean had spent almost his entire career at the college. As a graduating student in 1966, he was invited to join other staff taking part in the Great Proletarian Cultural

Revolution, a revolution devoted at our institute, Shen Yanbing once recalled, to struggle sessions, degradations, random violence and endless bickering. A decade later, he taught his first class—the institute was closed for six years, then served as a playground for the children of high officials—and he eventually was sent to the United States to improve his English. Dean Shen returned from America in 1982 to commence a meteoric rise within the department. He was loved by undergraduates for his sophistication but distrusted by colleagues for his scheming.

Among students that night, however, he was God, and the class monitor rightly begged him for a speech. Clutching a microphone that fed into the tape-player, the dean blasted greetings, tossed off a few uproarious jokes, and then, spotting Mary and me, conceded two sentences in English. Amid hurrahs, Shen Yanbing retired to a chair, where he was engulfed by delirious youth. The room abuzz, the monitor called for the rewind of a particularly snappy cassette. The festivities continued.

4

LEI FENG SPIRIT

i Feigan insisted on throwing the first dinner party. We would provide the opulent setting and quality facilities, and he the banquet. With other friends, we had usually managed to trick, plead or bully our way into paying the bulk of the expenses, especially meats and alcohol. Culinary pride required that a respectable menu include cold tidbits to start, beef, chicken and pork dishes, sautéed vegetables, seafood concoctions, dumplings or a fish and the obligatory closing soup. Add on bottles of beer, wine and soda, a selection of fruits and nuts for dessert, and the tab could climb distressingly near the monthly salary range ($20). We earned ten times the norm and could foot the bill without a thought as to how cash would be scrounged for next week's food tickets. Most people listened to reason, or else allowed themselves to be hoodwinked. Not Li Feigan, though. Never Li Feigan.

Li was, first of all, an older graduate student. The fruit of post-Liberation optimism and Maoist population practices, he grew up in time to be a sacrifice, albeit different from Dean Shen, to the lunacy of the Cultural Revolution. At age fourteen, Li was sent down to the countryside to learn from peasants how to break rocks. At twenty-two, rescued by deaths in high places, he crawled back to his hometown. Though to all intents and purposes written off by the state, Li wrote himself back in through intelligence, street savvy and a Sisyphus-like determination to keep pushing the boulder back up the hill. He gained entrance into a provincial college, excelled so blatantly that he was offered a teaching job, wooed a woman from among his students and worked patiently but persistently over a period of years toward a position in a master's program (nearly impossible) in Beijing (impossible). Li laughed off the wisdom that said he should accept a three-year separation from his wife with socialist self-abnegation (residency permits for the capital were not given out to the spouses of visiting outsiders, even if the "visit" lasted a decade) and blithely waged war on the bureaucracy for another year until he had secured her a place in a graduate program at a Beijing institute, not forty kilometers across town, not two bus rides away, but within walking distance of our campus. Li Feigan had been around (and around and around) and knew better than anyone else we encountered how to untie circles until they functioned as straight lines. It was, many claimed, a kind of magic.

Li was also from Shandong province, where the Yellow River joined the sea and the holy mountain Tai Shan nudged the heavens. Shandong was the country's cradle; kingdoms had risen and fallen there before other provinces even emerged from prehistory. Myths and legends were rooted in the province's rocky topsoil. Confucius was from Shandong, as was his disciple Mencius. Shandong men in 1990 were recognizably the same as their ancestors, who are immortalized in the fourteenth-century epic novel *Outlaws of the Marsh*. Honor, valor, revenge, violence: these were codes of conduct carved in flesh, sealed in blood. Shandong was also home to eighty million people, with a per capita income under $200 a year. During famine, the province was often hit first, and hardest. In remote areas, there were still no schools or electricity. Shandong supplied the army its most willing fodder, and construction sites in Shanghai and Beijing were rife with natives toiling twelve hours a day to mail money back to wives, kids, grandparents and grandchildren.

The hometown of Li Feigan was within biking distance of Confucius's residence and grave. This proximity lent the otherwise dusty industrial village of Jining an aura of ingrown scholasticism and statesmanship. Capable mandarins and astute business tycoons apparently grew on trees: something about the air, the local food, the trickle-down of a philosopher who had died barely twenty-five hundred years earlier. Li thought all that business was bunk and local cadres and wheeler-dealers beyond contempt. He had wanted out of Jining ever since discovering he was in it. Beijing was the only civilized place to live.

Dinner was at exactly six o'clock on Saturday. At two o'clock that afternoon, Li's wife, Dai Houxing, and a friend, Yu Wei, arrived laden with bags of uncooked edibles and special spices. Li himself had urgent business in the city but would be back in plenty of time. He appeared at 5:55 and helped arrange the cold dishes on the table. Even as a waiter, Li had a managerial comportment: crisp, precise, unperturbed by the loss of face implicit in service labor. Lesser men would have balked at the degradation. Li Feigan, though, understood the big picture, the pratfalls of hubris and the value of example.

His body brooked no excess or sloppiness. Trim and muscular, Li wore his poverty—he owned two pairs of pants, three shirts, a blue sports coat—with starched dignity and bleached pride. He exercised daily, abhorred smoking and washed his clothes beneath an open tap late at night. Li's mind was equally particular. His thinking was solid, an appealing blend of learning, tradition and experience. Ideas had beginnings, middles and ends for Li; problems were similarly containable, if only officials would stop being so retrograde. In careful English, he outlined solutions and envisioned reforms of matters ordinary (the pallid intellectual life on campus) and sublime (the ruling clique that was suffocating all hope). His specialty was the blueprint. Problem A could be solved by plan B, to be implemented in X stages over a period of Y years. Up the scale a little—from cafeteria food to, say, rural illiteracy—and Li simply fattened the figures, prolonged the gestation, measured increments in generations instead of decades. Conditions for change were often severe, and admissions of contingency, even flux, were readily offered. But failure was out of the question. Failure would not be tolerated.

Dinner was, happily, a success. Though Shandong cuisine was too salty for my taste, the meal was smooth and systematic, punctuated by good cheer. Plates of sliced potato with ginger, sweet water chestnuts, kelp and fermented eggs flowed into the main dishes of mushroom with pork, braised beef, chicken with onion and steaming bowls of dried-shrimp dumplings that we dipped in soy and vinegar. Diced apples and bananas followed, supplemented by coffee and chocolate Easter eggs (our contributions). Dai Houxing and Yu Wei did most of the serving, though Li disappeared into the kitchen at intervals to review the troops. Judging from his curt commands and the smile glued to Houxing's face, he was a stern master.

Our discomfort at the division of labor compelled me to toss out the current campus joke about community service. "Lei Feng spirit?" I said to Li, who was refilling glasses.

The women laughed.

"Not Lei Feng," he answered seriously. "Model Husband."

Lei Feng was a 1960s propaganda puppet, a foot soldier whose incessant self-denial and grinding patriotism—in his diary he described his lifelong ambition to be a "screw in the socialist machine"—bordered on the asinine. Felled by a telephone pole at a tender age, Lei Feng was quickly resurrected by the Party as the ideal citizen: passive, feckless, poised to jump out a window at the nod of a leader's head. In its senility, the government, rattled by the unruly ethos of the student movement, had recently dragged out its "Learn from Lei Feng" machine for yet another pacification campaign. Campus bulletin boards were dutifully splashed with the same photos and diary excerpts first used in 1965. The farce was self-evident— though Lei was "discovered" posthumously, a dozen shots of him engaged in selfless acts were available, along with the ruminations of a semiliterate recruit—and humiliating to intelligent people. He was presented as the exemplar for farmers, workers and intellectuals alike.

"Model Husband" was a trickier concept. I was one. I brewed Mary cups of tea. I made the bed. Sometimes I washed our clothes, cooked our meals. For many women, the status was one of grace: rare, precious, Western. But for others, and certainly the majority of men, the Model Husband was an ambiguous creature, part Buddha, part lapdog. The surface meaning was clear, but who trusted surfaces? The Model Husband was considerate (weak), willing to compromise (unmanly), unafraid of letting his feelings show (womanly). He, too, was worthy of emulation.

"Is Li a Model Husband?" I asked Houxing.

She smiled. Though ten years Li's junior, Dai Houxing was in many respects his match. Shy, quiet in both languages, she was also intelligent and perceptive, as sharp as Li in her thinking and considerably more acidic. Whether she deferred to him out of age, sex or respect, the fact was that she *did* defer, constantly. She was tall and thin, with an odd but striking face: long, thick cheekbones running in parallel lines to her chin, a wide mouth, small eyes. Houxing was a master's student in commerce and spoke English with the uncertainty of a provincial college graduate who has the sinking feeling that most of her teachers were themselves ill-taught in the language. She pondered my question.

"He *thinks* he is," she said.

"Not true," Li said. "Houxing tells me she does not want a Model Husband. I am only respecting her wishes."

"You don't want a Model Husband?" Mary asked her.

Houxing paused again. "I do not want what Li cannot give," she said simply.

That cracked the place up.

"I am misunderstood," Li complained.

"I think you are understood too well," I said.

Li grinned; he could take a joke. "Only Westerners can be Model Husbands," he said. "It is impossible for us to please our wives. They have seen too many foreign examples on television."

"I don't want my husband to act like a foreigner," Yu Wei said, adjusting her glasses. Yu Wei was also a graduate student, also in her thirties, and also from the countryside, Hubei province. She had a round face, weepy eyes and the stern expression of someone who has fretted too long over things that cannot be changed. One such imponderable was likely her husband, a sailor stationed at a naval installation near

Guangzhou, three thousand kilometers south of Beijing. Given that his term of duty extended to the year 2007, and that Wei would probably never receive permission to join him permanently, the man's comportment as spouse seemed a hypothetical matter.

"Why should we copy foreign models?" Yu Wei inquired.

"Because they are new," Houxing said, to everyone's surprise. "And *not* Lei Feng."

Li cleared his throat, leaning forward in his chair in the manner of a mandarin about to dispense wisdom. Heeding the signs, we all lowered our chopsticks and relaxed.

"There are many points to consider," he said. "The country needs models, of course. The old models, like the old ways of thinking, have been discredited, and people no longer take them seriously. But we must also remember that the outside world is different. Circumstances are not the same. Therefore, we must find internal solutions to internal problems. Also," Li continued, constructing his argument cautiously, as if shifts in national policy hung in the balance, "people resent those who copy the West. It is insulting to us, not in line with our national character. We must borrow from the outside without changing our behavior. We must learn Western technology—"

"What's wrong with changing your behavior?" I interrupted.

"People will be insulted."

"Why?"

"It is an imposition."

"Wu'er Kaixi insulted many people," Yu Wei offered. Wu'er Kaixi was one of the principal leaders of the student movement. His flamboyance and cocksure ways—dining with Western reporters, surrounding himself with an entourage—had once seemed dynamic; after the massacre, however, and Wu'er's flight to the United States, opinion had turned swiftly against him. He was a charlatan. He was a media puppet. Worse, he wasn't even Han in race: a Uygur, no less, member of some tribe that roamed the plains of central Asia.

"It is rumored," Wei said contemptuously, "that Wu'er was about to be expelled from Beijing Normal University for poor grades. He joined the demonstrations to avoid being sent home."

Yu Wei was a bitter person, easy to dismiss. Yet both Li and Houxing saw merit in her slander.

"Wu'er didn't respect people's patriotic feelings," Li said. "He acted too much like a foreigner."

"Like Zhou Shuren," Wei added.

"Zhou the film teacher?" I said.

"He is known to spend all his time with foreigners," Li explained. "During the Turmoil, he boasted that he knew journalists from *Newsweek* magazine and American newspapers. He is also openly critical of socialism with his students."

"He had a girlfriend at the Friendship Hotel," Wei said, referring to a massive foreigners-only apartment complex in northwest Beijing.

"A foreigner?" I asked innocently.

"French."

"How do you know this?"

"Zhou Shuren is famous on campus," Li said. "His arrest last year was much discussed. Zhou is an artist, and does not hide his scorn for scholars." Li's tone was genial; his words were not. There was an awkward silence. "Do you know Zhou?" he finally thought to ask.

"Yes."

"He is popular with—"

"Us. Right."

"What about Chai Ling?" Mary asked, wisely reverting to a national figure. "Is she okay?"

Chai Ling was another important student leader. She had vanished shortly before the crackdown, and rumors were still rife of safe-houses in the south, secret arrest and imprisonment in Qincheng, even reports that she and her husband were already in Hong Kong.

"Okay, yes," Houxing said.

"Chai Ling was too emotional," Li amended, unhappy with the subject. "She wept frequently and could not control her feelings."

"Men would never accept such a leader," Wei said. "A leader must be strong and dependable."

"She's very popular in Hong Kong," I said mischievously. "We bought a T-shirt there with her photo on it."

"Chai Ling lacks leadership skills," Li pronounced.

So much for Chai Ling. That left but one famous student activist. Han, male, bespectacled, incarcerated since July, Wang Dan was the people's choice as Model Revolutionary. I was about to mention his name when Mary, attentive to the mood of our guests, began clearing the table. Politeness panic set in as the five of us scrambled to grab plates, bowls, cups and bottles and charge the kitchen. Like most social occasions, dinners tended to break up suddenly, mysteriously, at the sound of a bell no Westerner could hear. Anticipating a swift closure, I unfolded a sheet of calligraphy sent to us by a friend in the south. Six columns of ideographs, the two left rows shorter by half, created a stately visual play between black line and white space. The calligraphy was rigid, painted with a stiff brush. Neither Mary nor I could read very well and sought help.

"It looks old," Houxing said.

"Hard to understand," Li agreed.

"Is the script ancient?" I asked.

Li bent over the sheet, his brow furrowing in concentration. He cleared his throat again. "I cannot read many of the characters," he said. "The calligraphy is poor. Was this done by a foreigner?"

"What?"

"The lines are shaky."

"Why does that mean—?"

"Not a foreigner," Houxing interjected. "Very old. Maybe Tang dynasty."

"Maybe earlier," Wei said. "Sui dynasty."

"Maybe it's Confucius," I said.

In the hall, Li abruptly changed topics. "Our economic and social problems are not so easily solved," he said. "It will take years to educate the population so they may participate in a more democratic system of government."

Why was he telling me this?

"Though it is still helpful to discuss our difficulties with experts from other countries," Li went on, "we must be prepared to deal with matters by ourselves. The biggest problem is education."

"Of the peasants?" I said, familiar with both the jargon and the argument.

"The billion people in the countryside have not received enough education. Without their support, reforms are impossible—progress is inconceivable. We must, therefore, reform our education system thoroughly, in order to make the peasants better informed and better able to conceive of political change."

We all looked like mourners at a funeral: eyes lowered, shifting from foot to foot in the doorway. But Li wasn't finished. "The reforms will take a long time," he said, beads of sweat sprouting on his forehead.

"Generations?" I guessed.

"It must be gradual, a natural evolution. Radical change only leads to instability, which causes chaos."

I got it, finally. Li had been dying to lecture me since they'd arrived. "Chaos like last May and June?" I inquired.

"The Turmoil was the result of impatience."

I waited.

"The students failed to acknowledge the significant changes taking place in our society. Perhaps these changes were not obvious, but they were solid and substantial. Students wanted everything to happen instantly, like on television. Their impatience created instability."

"The soldiers may have had something to do with it," Mary said.

"Of course. But the Turmoil was only the result of a mistake made by—" Li stopped abruptly. Houxing's face, until recently red, had just deepened to crimson, and her smile had long vanished. Never had I witnessed such open, if mute, dissent. Neither had Li, apparently; he blanched, then gathered the women's coats. To lessen the tension, I deemed his gallantry to be model, not specifying which variety. Yu Wei suggested a compromise: "Model Citizen." Li Feigan was a Model Citizen. We were all Model Husbands and Wives. We were all Lei Fengs.

Zhou Shuren wasn't a Lei Feng. He never swept floors, scrubbed sinks, washed windows or in any other way participated in the maintenance of communal spaces. Zhou shared a room on the third floor of a dormitory that had once housed foreign students but was currently home to young teachers. A year ago, the halls had been bright and airy, kept slick by staff who equated a wet surface with a clean surface and left mop trails wherever they roamed. Now, plunged into perpetual dimness by burnt-out light bulbs, the stairwells were open wounds—peeling paint, bruises from bicycles—and landings featured garbage drumlins in the corners. Hallways were equally filthy, the air rank with in-room cooking odors and the stench of toilets.

Thirty teachers shared a corridor. The majority of these people dozed through political studies meetings together and exchanged magazines during departmental snoozes, with the lucky one in twenty-five selected for membership in the Communist Party earning the right to sit at stiff attention at those assemblies. Meetings were the proprietors of afternoons. Meetings *owned* the corporal self; attendance was mandatory, absence punishable by fines and scoldings. Though officially the forum for thrashing out the self-evident truths of the system (comradeship, cooperation, the dictatorship of the proletariat), meetings were actually about body counts (solidarity in statistical bulk, unity in the sharing of oxygen). Zhou Shuren, for example, once attempted to evoke the cooperation principle by suggesting a meeting of dormitory residents to organize a cleaning schedule. If each occupant did one or two chores a week—swept a floor, cleaned a basin— and pitched in a few *jiao* to buy light bulbs, the building would be restored to decency. Colleagues laughed in Zhou's face. Cleaning corridors was not their responsibility. Changing light bulbs fell outside their jurisdiction. No one had ordered them to do it. No one had proclaimed a campaign. As for convening an unofficial, unaffiliated meeting to discuss the matter, the concept was offensive. Was Zhou Shuren playing the big shot? People wouldn't stand for the pretense. But no, Zhou was just being weird, under the influence of Tiananmen, foreigners, rock and roll.

I climbed the tenement to his room. Bicycle phantoms loomed in the stairwell and a smell, sharpened by the frigid air, flared my nostrils. Room numbers were cloaked in darkness, forcing me to linger outside each door to decipher the name tag. Slants of interior light that escaped under frames and between joints illuminated the mounds of garbage that were decomposing in the corridor. I stumbled over a wok left to cool, causing a racket. In spite of the cold, the last room on the floor was open, door ajar. Music blared into the public domain: Bruce Springsteen, of all people, the acoustic dirges of *Nebraska*. Shivering, my breath a funnel of steam, I listened to a verse of "Atlantic City":

> "Everything dies baby that's a fact
> But maybe everything that dies someday
> comes back."

Zhou was slow to answer my knock. Either he had just woken up or else he had been weeping.

"Where is Atlantic City?" he asked huskily, scrubbing his face with his hands.

"Far away," I answered.

"I want to go there," he said.

Zhou's room was half a room. He shared it with a former student and teacher at the college who was now employed in private business. Which business, and why the man was able to retain accommodation on campus, were mysteries that Zhou was certain he could explain: the roommate was a spy, planted to incriminate him.

Rumor had it that the Party had issued a quota for each Beijing work unit: 1 percent of staff had to be punished for participation in the Turmoil. It was a modest figure, compared with previous purges. Still, if the actual number of troublemakers was, say, 3 percent, the process would single out the weakest. If the reality was that no one in the work unit had done anything wrong, then villains would have to be fabricated. Complicating the algebra at our institute—a minor player in the movement—was the fact that a solid quarter of the student body and perhaps a tenth of the faculty, not to mention administrative staff, had marched in at least one demonstration. How to select? Zhou Shuren believed he had already been pegged as the school's Isaac. The roommate, a friendly if oafish man who smiled incessantly and cluttered the walls with pinups from Taiwan, was to be his Abraham, and in the Marxist lexicon, divine intervention would only make matters worse.

Zhou had no choice but to coexist with his betrayer. Close quarters heightened the tension; the roommate rarely showered, never changed his bedding or washed his clothes. The roommate, Zhou summarized, like the teachers in the corridor who had refused to endorse his cleanup campaign, like everyone at the institute, was a pig. His rancor, delivered in a bleary whisper—the man was in the room—fizzled into silence.

"Can your roommate speak English?" I asked.

"He claims not," Zhou answered. "But he is lying."

"What should we do?" I asked.

"It doesn't matter," he sighed. "They know already."

Though barely two meters away from us, the roommate was still a wall apart. The wall comprised three panels normally used to subdivide classrooms. Zhou had borrowed the panels last September and erected, to the protest and embarrassment of the roommate, a partition down the center of the four-meter by three-meter chamber. His half opened onto the door, meaning he could come and go, eat and sleep, without ever seeing the human being who lived within arm's reach. Zhou had even put up a curtain to prevent unwanted sightings when the man entered or exited. Belches and coughs, smacks and snores, were conjectural: the roommate was a ghost, and could easily—if all one's concentration were focused on it—be ignored.

"Does he mind you leaving the door open?" I asked.

"Does who mind?" Zhou replied.

"How does he feel about Bruce Springsteen?" I wondered.

"How does who feel?" Zhou said.

That settled, I sat on a chair at the foot of the bed. Zhou's half room had a bed, two chairs, a bookshelf, a desk. Also a tape-player, drawers of cassettes and a borrowed guitar that he liked to strum. Along the partition were posters of the plays that Zhou had performed in, art exhibitions he had helped organize and a British film in which he had once landed a tiny part, thanks to his slangy English. He acted in one ten-second scene and spoke eight words of dialogue. In the scene, Zhou, marching in a Red Guard rally, counsels a curious bystander: "Join the revolution, comrade, or else fuck off!" If ever a part meshed with an actor's inclinations, this was it. Zhou recalled with fondness the shoot, the crew and most especially his contribution to the universal understanding of Mao's principle of Perpetual Revolution.

"It was great," he commented. "Free food and beer on the set."

"How long did you rehearse the line?" I asked.

"Six weeks," Zhou said. "Day and night: in class, on buses, while walking along the street."

Scriptwriters had debated different versions of the speech. He listed the other finalists:

1. "Join in our glorious revolution, friend, or else go
fuck yourself and your family!" (too wordy)

2. "Help fight against the Liu Shaoqi clique, comrade, or
else be a running dog!" (too theoretical)

3. "Support the Great Helmsman and the revolution,
brother, or else I'll smash your fucking face in!" (too
individualistic)

The winning line combined, it was felt, all the sensitivity and idealism of a Red Guard going forth to abuse and denigrate for the glory of the Supreme Ruler. Zhou supported the decision and hissed his phrase into the camera. The moment was transcendent and now, five years on, burned in Zhou's memory with a fervor equaled by only one other event in his life: a three-month trek in Tibet.

We ended up talking about Tibet. In a frigid monk's cell—both of us wore coats and gloves in recognition of the official March 15 "end of winter," and of heat, announced yesterday—lit by a sallow bulb, with *Nebraska* in the background and the rustlings of potential betrayal audible through the partition, Zhou alternated gulps of beer ("Who needs a fridge?" he said, clutching a cold bottle) with slurred ruminations on freedom and constriction, on getting lost in Tibet, on his own out-of-body experience on a slope of Mount Everest, and on the reports of a friend who, sought by police for Tiananmen activities, had vanished into the celestial desolation of the central Asian plateau, source of both the Yellow and Yangtze rivers, edge of the world (though actually the belly of it), where no one knew anyone or knew anything *about* anyone except themselves, and where loneliness was redundant—Can a mountain be lonely? Can the wind lack companionship?—and the self, the prison of consciousness, was so superfluous, so unhelpful, that it eventually faded, like an echo; and Zhou rambled on about his friend, an artist, who was handed a video camera free of charge by a fleeing German tourist last June, and who then escaped Beijing for northern Tibet, surviving a forty-day trek into the heart of the country, an unnamed village in an unidentified valley in a range of mountains distinguished on topographical maps by only a number. There, the friend was making films with the video camera, writing books with a pencil, living like a reasonably free man in a reasonably free nation, devoid, significantly, of both human life and governments. Zhou should be making films in an unidentified valley. Zhou should be writing books in an unnamed village. Beijing was killing him. The college would be his demise.

"Join the revolution, comrade, or else fuck off!" I said, buttoning my coat. It was late.

He accompanied me into the hallway, taking my arm in support. Behind us the roommate coughed and rustled his betrayal, or possibly just a newspaper.

"Meet me in Atlantic City," Zhou said in a strange voice.

5

BASKETBALL

By late March, I was once again playing basketball outdoors. Most afternoons it was cold and windy; players wore sweaters and insulated track pants, puffed like steam engines and chain-smoked to ensure that at least their lungs stayed warm. But they came out regularly, and asked me to come out, and looked puzzled when I complained about the weather.

The institute had only two courts. Both were ravaged: cracked and uneven cement, splintery wooden backboards, bent rims, no mesh. Basketballs themselves were scarce, and tended to bounce too much, bounce too little, or else had long ago lost their grip and become hard beach balls. The best rim on the best half court was reserved for "the Big Game," a daily assembly—four o'clock in spring and fall, early evening during the blistering summer months—of the seasoned, the battered, the washed-up. Few undergraduates played. Young men were too skittish; lacking skills, they reverted to bumps and shoves, fouls so flagrant no one even bothered to call them. The bulk of the regulars were faculty, phys-ed teachers and people who lived in campus housing but worked elsewhere. A typical team might contain an economics professor, a librarian, a cook, a foreigner. The mix was ecumenical, a crisscross of classes and races that would have caused a scandal off court. Though foursomes were occasionally selected, most often they simply evolved on the basis of who was present, had changed their shoes, finished their cigarette. Built into the system was a safeguard against grandstanding and excess favoritism. Losing teams had to quit the court and winners wore down eventually. Nothing lasted forever in pickup basketball.

One of my favorite players was Li Feigan, a classic point guard with good ball-handling skills, an excellent outside shot and the sixth sense of a natural playmaker. Li saw the court, and the movements of teammates, in perpetual future tense: the cut a man *might* make, the hole that *might* open if two, three, four conditions were met. Better than anyone else, Li could will a rhythm into a match, distribute the shots, goad lethargic bodies into following a pass and discipline those who lagged. He was definitely the boss; anyone with an instinct for the game, or anyone who just wanted to touch the ball, had better recognize the fact.

I preferred teaming up with older men. Though a step slower and reluctant to hustle back on defense, these athletes were cool and collected, less prone to silly mistakes or ego trips. For undergraduates, discipline of any kind was an imposition. Mandatory physical-education classes persisted at the college level. Twice weekly, from 3:00 to 4:00 P.M., twenty-year-olds were subjected to lessons in sports that more than likely did not interest them. After four o'clock, however, they were free to choose their own activities and, like pistons fired by suppressed nervous tension, these students raced up and down the court and pounced all over one another. To possess the basketball was to possess a means of self-expression; to relinquish it, therefore, was madness, and the three arm-waving teammates could go to hell. One side of the brain informed them that the discipline of team athletics was *not* the discipline of socialist living, but the other side said, Fuck it, I have the ball, the ball goes in the basket, don't ask me for it, don't tell me where to pass it, fuck you, fuck everyone, wildness must be freedom, adrenaline must be hope. Undergraduates made lousy teammates.

Older players knew better. Perhaps former Red Guards, perhaps teenagers during the fatuous "To Get Rich Is Glorious" campaigns of the early 1980s, these men had long since given up expelling anger physically. Positions, patterns, even plays had ceased to be restrictions and insults; as athletes, they had acquired wisdom at the expense of hope. They were mild and sad, and played the game fairly well, fairly consistently, executing simple cuts and making routine shots without fuss or fanfare. A nifty pass or a sharp move met with restrained praise, a handshake. Players knew they were good, knew that basketball allowed them to create, modestly, to express an inner life, modestly, and that the sport *did* mean something, however ephemeral.

One regular was a handsome man in his twenties who played in black slippers and a blue track suit. He would stop by the court on the way back from the city, shoot a few balls, then stroll home to change. His day uniform—a coat and tie—was rare enough to prompt me to ask about him. Another player, a political science teacher named Li Qiubai, was happy to answer my query.

"The guy is Public Security," he said of the well-dressed athlete. "Jiang Wenyuan is his name. When he wears nice clothes it means he is working undercover. Like James Bond," Li added.

"He looks young," I said.

"Twenty-three. Last year he received a promotion for his excellent work during the Turmoil. Now he trains other secret police."

"He spies on students?"

"Right."

"But he lives on a university campus?"

"Close to the action," Li said dryly. Besides sports, Li Qiubai also loved action-and-adventure movies: Clint Eastwood, Arnold Schwarzenegger, madcap cop flicks from Hong Kong. "Jiang's mother works in the administration office. His father was destroyed during the Cultural Revolution."

I failed to hide my dismay. "Was he on campus during the student movement?" I asked.

"He marched with our school along Chang'an Avenue to Tiananmen Square, and took many photos as 'souvenirs.' Jiang also slept on the square with students from outside Beijing to collect their names and hometowns. His work was outstanding, you see. That is why he now wears a suit."

"I can't believe it."

"What is there not to believe?"

"But he *spies* on you?"

"Not on me," he answered. "Others. Troublemakers and counter-revolutionaries. Besides, Jiang has a good job. Good salary and benefits. Money to buy nice clothes and eat in restaurants. Not like us teachers."

I gaped, but Li Qiubai only shrugged and threw up a shot. It went in; he was a dead-eye from the right baseline.

I knew little about the Public Security Bureau (*Gongan* according to the pinyin on the doors of their vehicles) except that they shared with the Communist Party the honor of being most responsible, day to day, for the welfare of an authoritarian state. Rumored to number in the tens of thousands in Beijing alone, the secretive PSB preferred plainclothes to uniforms and intimidation to blunt violence (with frequent exceptions). Though its functions were various, including traffic control and the investigation of ordinary offenses, the bureau's specialty was the political crime, a violation of such ambiguity it meant nothing, or everything, and affected no one, or everyone, and was the activity of a few deviants, or of the entire population. Undercover police were ubiquitous at official gatherings, around government buildings and international hotels, in parks and squares, and though they were often recognizable by their starched white shirts and cold stares (locals usually knew whom to steer clear of), they were supposed to be invisible, sensed in a pressure at the back of the skull, a nervous glance over the shoulder.

My head was certainly throbbing when our local cop showed up at the court wearing new Nike basketball shoes, worth one hundred *yuan* on Wangfujing Street. The man smiled at the assembled, cracked a joke. During the game I elbowed him, stepped over his sneakers and made sure to follow through on blocked shots with my full weight, knocking him down twice. Jiang Wenyuan bloodied his knee but bounced back up both times. I wanted the other players to know what he was, to know that I knew what he was, and to join me in ridding the game of a worm. I wanted mob justice. I wanted revenge.

But no one caught on. And Jiang Wenyuan, who was either wily or genuinely unaware, absorbed my fury with good nature; the sport was physical, players bumped, no harm done. Only once did he make eye contact with me, briefly, his expression unreadable. He kept returning to play. I kept returning to play. We all kept returning to the single decent court with the single decent ball and the dozen or so decent athletes. Jiang-the-secret-policeman was a good player, too, with a solid jump shot and a strong move to the basket. Also, as the weeks passed, I noticed more and more how thin, almost fragile, he was. He coughed, rubbed bloodshot eyes, tired before the others. He could have been a malnourished undergraduate. He could have been an earnest scholar starving on a pitiful monthly stipend.

One afternoon we decided to divide up into three four-man squads. I was asked to select a fourth member for our team, and Jiang Wenyuan was the best choice left. Still I hesitated. How could I? How could anyone? Li Qiubai nudged me impatiently. Jiang stood with his arms folded, Nikes already scuffed, and smiled directly at me, at the others, at no one at all. Like confetti into the air, I threw up my certainties, renounced my status, abandoned my privileges and called his name.

Jiang Wenyuan made several excellent passes during the game. Our team won three times in a row.

The *lianhefangwei* brigade was patrolling the track one evening in March, undeterred by icy sleet and a socked-in sky that paralyzed thoughts of spring. Old ladies wearing puffed Mao suits and yellow armbands that granted them license to meddle, these voluntary PSB agents combed the campus daily with squinting eyes and tut-tutting mouths. In the Qing dynasty the *baojia*, a community mutual responsibility system, would execute a wife for her husband's crimes and banish neighbors for the indiscretions of the family next door. Everyone was responsible; everyone, therefore, kept everyone else in line. Snooping, slandering, even dispensing mob justice became acts of survival, with plenty of leeway for vengeance and cruelty. Modern tattle mills played down the violence—neighborhood watches were supposed to concentrate on deterring robbers—while remaining devoted to innuendo and casual suspicion. Class struggle in the 1980s still urged the citizen to invade privacy in pursuit of errant behavior and the enemies of socialism. Such contributions to the social fabric met with praise and promotion. That, at least, was the theory. In practice, neighborhood watches gave old people something to do all day, while simultaneously upholding abstract tenets of exclusion in order that national stability, forever prey to the dogs of anarchy, could be maintained.

Members of the watch, whose mandate since the Turmoil had emphasized the ferreting-out of suspicious overnight visitors within their precinct (in many Beijing districts it was a crime not to report a guest to the *lianhefangwei*), sat on a bench husking sunflower seeds with their teeth and chattering. One woman held what looked like a wool egg in her arms (spies often doubled as baby-sitters) and attention had temporarily shifted from defending the country to cooing and trilling over a swaddled grandchild. I slipped past this menacing brood and entered the track for a brisk stroll. Guo Yidong, just completing his sixth lap, was happy for the company.

"It's raining," I offered. "It's raining, and you look soaked."

Guo asked for a more precise term to describe the weather. "Given the thickness of the, ahem, drops," he said, "and their horizontal paths, is 'rain' the best word?"

"Sleet," I corrected. "This awful stuff is sleet."

"Not hail?" he wondered.

"Not yet," I answered. "But there's hope for hail as well."

Guo loved the patina of "sleet." He repeated the word, reveling in the contortions his mouth had to perform to pronounce it. I had a question about sleet. "All things are connected?" I began.

"Correct," Guo replied.

"According to traditional medicine," I continued, "phenomena—physical, spiritual, even intellectual—cannot exist independently of each other?"

"Nothing survives in isolation," he agreed.

"Okay," I said, pleased by the shape of my argument. "Do you have a cold?"

"Right now?" he said, coughing.

"Right this very instant," I confirmed.

He stopped to ponder. Lacking the shield of glasses, Guo's eyes had withdrawn to the back of his head; his sockets resembled swollen bee-stings. When he raised his hand to rub the sores, much of his glove had unraveled and some fingers were bare.

"I believe I do have a cold," he finally said.

"And are you taking medicine for it?"

"Traditional remedies."

"And are you staying in bed and resting?"

"My afternoon nap is longer than usual."

"And are you avoiding getting chilled and damp and thoroughly soaked?" I queried with a smile. Guo smiled also. I waited. Guo waited also.

"Well?" I said.

"It is, let me see, a mental condition," he eventually replied.

"*What's* a mental condition?" I asked, already knowing.

"My physical state," Guo said. "External symptoms mirror the internal illness, which must be cured first. The weather is, ahem, irrelevant to my health."

"If walking in freezing sleet for an hour isn't relevant to your health," I said, "what is?"

Guo confessed to an incomplete self-diagnosis, a source of considerable mental disquiet that necessitated, somewhat ironically, longer and more frequent strolls through the assorted meteorological fronts that were assailing the city like the plagues of Moses. I suggested that he recover from his malady first, and *then* get his philosophical house in order. I even offered Western medicines from our cabinet: cold tablets, throat lozenges, cough syrup. Guo was polite but dismissive.

"Western medicines cure the illness," he explained for the umpteenth time. "Traditional medicines prevent it." Though I saw holes in his thinking—like his disintegrating gloves and torn jacket, the cracks in the soles of his shoes that had been stuffed with newspaper—I dropped the subject, except to express concern for his health.

"We are taught to expect little and to get less," Guo said suddenly. "Our national character has been defined by limitation—we do as we're told." The shift in topic was bewildering.

"Do you believe in a national character?" I inquired.

Guo hiccuped at the question. "I would rather not," he replied. "Taoism advises that the individual be true only to his inner life. A person belongs to no one—not a family, city, not even a country. He should, in consequence, be free of national characteristics. But," Guo added, clasping his hands behind his back in scholarly concentration, "I worry that I am a failure as an individual. I reflect too many qualities of my, ahem, what is another word for living conditions?"

"Environment?"

"Environment, yes. This is a weakness. My environment has defined me too forcibly. In a sense, environment limits the ability to achieve self-knowledge. Failure of personality becomes inevitable, makes it, could I say, in actual fact a failure of character ..." Again he hiccuped, likely in surprise at his own ideas.

We were silent for a moment. Two loops around the track were ample; the sky was coal black, the sleet still spat, and even the grandmotherly snoops had retreated indoors. When Guo sighed, a rare expression of emotion, I hastened to speak.

"Nobody escapes it, Guo," I said. "We're all from someplace."

"Of course," he answered. "I mention the issue in the spirit of discussion."

On the way to his room for a badly needed cup of tea, I asked Guo to elaborate on his enigmatic earlier statement.

"The 'little' we expect," he said, "is health and security. The 'less' we receive is poor health and, ahem, contingency."

"Because of national characteristics?" I said.

"I blame no one but myself," he replied.

6

SHU SHEYU

S hu Sheyu was a cripple. Childhood polio had seen to that; his left leg was a disaster, knee permanently swollen, foot crooked inward like a field hockey stick. Muscle refused to adhere to such paltry bones, leaving the limb pallid and wiry. Though Shu was otherwise extremely fit, broad shouldered and muscular, and was an excellent athlete, accomplished at basketball, soccer and table tennis, and was certainly the handsomest man we knew, not to mention the brightest, most talented—despite these attributes, he remained, categorically, to the exclusion of all else, a cripple. Around campus he was generally known simply as "the cripple," an epithet delivered aloud without the slightest trace of embarrassment. The term was, apparently, mere description. Whether out of resignation, disgust or mischief, Shu countered with his own response. During the opening ceremony of an intramural track meet, parading around the loop with the tiny contingent from the history department, he proudly displayed a placard describing the section as "An Old Man, a Woman and the Cripple." He ran in the four-hundred-meter race. Nearing the finish line, a solid minute behind the rest of the heat—no amount of technique or determination could cancel a bum leg—Shu broke into a grin and, turning to the bleachers, offered a flawless imitation of a champion surging toward the red tape, chest thrust out, features wrenched, arms raised in exultation. The crowd loved it, and Shu was awarded a special medal for sportsmanship.

Being a cripple exempted Shu from a straitjacket of responsibilities. Activities, attitudes, even public pronouncements that would have been censured in anyone else went unremarked and seemingly uncriticized. His physical dysfunction rendered him not only marginal but harmless—a situation that Shu relished. As a teacher, he flouted pedagogic convention, lecturing "Western style," with lots of movement around the hall, gimmicky visual aids and direct questions to stimulate discussion, while peppering dry redactions of officially sanctioned reality with doses of irony and parallelism. Like many scholars, Shu had been transformed by the 1987 television series "River Elegy," an iconoclastic exploration of the national heritage and the dead weight of millennia of continuous history using the Yellow River as a metaphor. Unlike others, however, he continued to teach the series—denounced after Tiananmen, its makers exiled or arrested—in the winter of 1989–90, achieving the lauded, but usually fatal, status of rebel simply by speaking in a normal voice while those around him were whispering. Yet Shu taught the disgraced material with impunity.

His personal life was equally intemperate. Shu dwelt with a half dozen other teachers on the top floor of an administrative building that was desolate after hours. He lived alone in a spacious room—compensation for his handicap—that had been divided, again using "borrowed" partitions, into a sleeping area at the back and a larger dining space decorated with liquor bottles and posters of Hong Kong starlets. During one social event, Shu shrouded the single light bulb that dangled over a table with purple rice paper. The purplish light, the tang of cigarette smoke, the chatter of titillated revelers and throb of disco music on a faltering tape deck lent the scene an aura of exoticism and sexual tension. Life in all its natural complexity was being lived inside Shu's room. What went on behind the door was, of course, less than tumultuous: daily gatherings of fellow teachers to cook on his hot plate, occasional dinners attended by foreigners and the rare unbridled party where Shu's groupies—undergraduate girls who doted on him as they would a kindly uncle—giggled amid an assembly of professors, graduate students and dangerous-looking men from outside campus who sported mirrored sunglasses, despite the purple light. It was the *potential* for emotional complexity that made events in Shu's room so electric, and so real. That Shu Sheyu would hold parties that extended beyond the eleven o'clock curfew (everyone on campus, including us, was locked into, or out of, their dormitories at this hour) and dared to invite various species of animal life to attend, and encouraged the adoration of teenage girls was, or should have been, sensational stuff. But his escapades remained stubbornly feckless, the eccentricities of a fringe element—hardly cause for concern.

Shu's Rabelaisian appetites peaked around foreigners. He loved food, all food; loved alcohol, all alcohol, but especially American bourbon; loved to watch TV, almost all programs, but particularly dubbed American dramas; loved to drop by for fifteen minutes and then stay for hours, just sitting and talking, or sitting and not talking. To chat on the phone was also a pleasure. Students and young staff, a total of two thousand people, had access to six telephones, so Shu often showed up at our door only to spend the next hour shouting into the receiver. The trick was not minding. Even during a formal "visit," Shu expected to be ignored, expected us to go about our business, even to go out altogether, while he ate our food, drank our liquor, toyed with the gadgets that littered the apartment. Once the ground rules were established, he proved an amiable guest, easy to invite and easy to throw out (he didn't mind), an excellent chef, good translator of television news and an engaging conversationalist. His interests, besides history, ranged from literature (he had read the epics by the age of twelve and knew Tang dynasty poems and passages of Lu Xun and Lao She by heart) through architecture to women's fashion, a subject he spoke volubly on one evening after lowering the level of a bottle of bourbon by three inches. Shu Sheyu was a blackguard and a chancer, a Dickens character adrift in a propaganda pamphlet glorifying a faceless society.

He was also a twenty-eight-year-old man whose experience of women, undergraduate entourages aside, had been limited, perhaps nonexistent. Whatever the reason, and suspecting the bad leg seemed reasonable, Shu was perpetually alone and without romantic prospects. Little wonder, then, at my shock and delight the afternoon of April 1 when he announced that he'd had a date the night before.

Shu was foraging in the refrigerator, dressed in glitzy clothes—a purple-and-black tracksuit, high-top running shoes—that his younger brother, a student in Shanghai who dabbled in black-market activities, had bought for him. Not until he had selected a bottle of beer, opened it with his mouth (a ghastly trick he insisted on performing) and plunked himself down on the living room couch before a bowl of peanuts did he deign to provide the details he knew I was dying to hear.

"A date," Shu confirmed in his meticulous English. "With a girl."

"Which girl?"

"A second-year student."

"History department?"

"She studies English. Also, she is a track-and-field specialist. Running, and the long jump."

He drank off a glass, nonchalant.

"And ...?" I said.

"And what?"

"Her name, Shu."

"Cathy."

"Cathy?"

"Her English name is Cathy."

"What about her real name?"

"Li Wei."

"And you asked her out on a date?"

Savoring the moment, Shu inquired if we had any chocolate Easter eggs left. I ignored the question. He emptied the beer bottle. "She invited me," he said simply.

"Li Wei asked *you* on a date?"

"To have a yogurt."

"In the cafeteria?"

64

"Yesterday afternoon," he said. "She came up to me outside the teaching building and said, 'Mr. Shu, are you available for a yogurt this evening?'"

"Nice."

"She is a nice girl. We talked for maybe two hours. She is smart, and also beautiful."

"But you met in the cafeteria?" I repeated.

"Naturally."

"And people saw you?"

"It was crowded with students drinking sodas and eating sunflower seeds. Also, many people pick up bottles of milk after dinner."

Campus courtship decorum, a rigid if unwritten code, ranked meeting together in a public place high on the scale of romantic attachments. Individuals were immediately designated a couple, and a couple was a social unit above its component parts. Obligations, pressures, standards to be upheld loomed large before the lovers, most likely still mere acquaintances. The desire for privacy in relationships, a leitmotif of almost all complaints, was interpreted by the collective as either the arrogant and selfish hunger for secrecy, or else a smoke screen for illicit carryings-on. It was not tolerated, and was in any event virtually impossible in an environment where gossip constituted the sole acceptable form of social interaction between authority-fearing people. More than once, friends confessed their despair over the lack of privacy in their lives, only to turn around and gossip relentlessly about other friends and colleagues, particularly those rumored to be hiding something—a lover, a second job, an application to an American university. Shu and Li Wei became an item, and an extraordinary one, within seconds of pulling out cafeteria stools.

"Li Wei bought the yogurts," Shu added casually.

"Wow," I said.

"She is a feminist."

I was speechless.

"Very interesting girl," he agreed, coming close to blushing. "She has many ideas about men and women, and her teachers say that she asks questions in class. I think this is good."

"And she runs and jumps?"

"One-hundred meter, two-hundred meter, and the long jump. She finished second in Liaoning province in middle school and will represent our college at a competition in June."

Shu got himself another beer. I asked him to put the kettle on, and he spent the next ten minutes fiddling with the stove before returning to the living room with a bottle, a teapot and a cup. He was in no rush.

"People must be talking about you," I said.

"I don't care."

"Especially if they saw the woman buy the yogurts. That's pretty scandalous, isn't it?"

"Maybe," he answered tersely. Then, after a silence, he said, "The word *ren* means 'human being' but also 'all people.' The character—" Shu sketched the character in his left palm "— contains both 'man' and 'two' in its strokes, meaning that a person can only be defined by his relationship with others. No one is allowed to be alone."

"Do people want to be alone?"

"They don't want to be bothered."

"Is that the same thing?"

"Perhaps not," he said. Shu was quiet for a minute, his eyelids blinking like a machine that counted thoughts. Generally as animated as the opera masks he loved, Shu's face in repose was even more extraordinary. The hugeness of his features—forehead, eyes, cheekbones, everything except the nose seemed oversized—bestowed a quality that more homogeneous, and therefore more "beautiful," faces lacked: personality.

"People want to be bothered by friends and family, nothing else. Without family, we feel empty and hollow. But everyone also complains that there are too many people in the country and it is impossible to ever be alone. Hard to understand," he admitted.

"There's such an awareness of race," I said. "Everyone is so political."

"No one I know is political."

"You are."

"I hate politics," Shu said.

"We're talking politics right now."

"No."

"No?"

"Politics is something else," he insisted, pouring tea into his beer glass. "Politics is an imposition, what is forced upon us. It is never a voluntary action."

"But your lives——?"

"Those are our lives," he interrupted. "Not us."

I kept quiet.

"I am speaking about personal issues, all that really matters to people. Everyone wants only a private life, but everyone has only a public life. If we find a person who *has* a full personal life, we get angry and jealous and try to destroy it. But," he said, "I don't care about any of this. I ignore gossip. I live like I want to."

"Li Wei does too," I said.

Shu beamed. "She is an interesting girl," he said.

I chanced upon a private connection between subjects, and, it being Shu Sheyu, I decided to give it a go. "Did you know there's a secret policeman living on campus?" I asked.

"Which one?"

"Which one??"

"There are many policemen at the institute. Workers in the foreigners' building are often undercover agents."

"The basketball player ..." I said numbly.

"Jiang Wenyuan?" Shu said. "His mother is employed by the administration. Her office is located on the floor below my room. When the window is open I hear her singing quite clearly."

"Does she have a nice voice?"

"She is from Sichuan and sings in dialect. I am familiar with the melodies but don't understand many of the words. Jiang's father was killed in a battle between Beijing Red Guards," he added.

"Do you know Jiang Wenyuan?"

"I know *of* him."

"Do you know that he informed on students who attended the demonstrations last spring?" I said, my voice rising. "That he marched into the city with the college and took photos, copied down names?"

Shu laughed bitterly, his only comment.

I moved on to the official purpose of his visit: a dinner party planned for next week. Though the convenient day for everybody was Wednesday, I kept offering Shu an alternative: Wednesday was the eve of Qingming Festival, the traditional day of mourning for the dead. In recent history, Qingming had proved incendiary, an occasion for the airing of grievances and agendas. During one festival, in 1976, public expressions of grief had sparked a government crackdown. Rumors that families of victims of the massacre would attempt to lay wreaths on Tiananmen Square were rampant, and many people, including us, were unnerved by the prospect of being exhumed from the winter's deep freeze. Hosting a dinner the night before what might prove the first in a sequence of protests leading up to the June 4 anniversary seemed unwise.

But Shu was adamant. "Wednesday is good," he said. "No one will be allowed to mourn on Qingming. No one will be allowed to show respect for the dead, except inside our houses with the curtains drawn across the windows."

We agreed on a time. Shu had an evening class to teach—a private history course he gave to some French students—and rose to leave. Besides English and French, he was now also studying a third foreign language.

"You know Joseph?" Shu began, referring to a banker friend who, though half-Japanese and half-American, had been raised in Copenhagen and now represented a Danish bank in Beijing. "Joseph is helping me get a visa to study in Copenhagen. But I must learn to speak Danish in order to go to school there."

"You're taking Danish lessons?"

"From Joseph's sister. She also works for the bank." Shu offered a sentence of his new tongue, then translated, "*Wo xuexi Helianyu.*"

"'I am studying Danish,'" I said in English.

"Slowly," he added. On his way out, Shu stopped in the kitchen to pluck an orange from a basket. "I'm also reading a banned book," he said, peeling the fruit. "By the American Zbigniew Brzezinski. It is about the failure of world communism. The translation was prepared for high Party officials only."

"How did you get hold of it?"

"From a friend."

"How did the friend—?"

"His father."

"Who's his father?"

"He works at the Great Wall–Sheraton Hotel."

"Is Brzezinski's book interesting?" I asked.

"Very," Shu answered, tossing peels onto the table. "I do not agree with all he says, but I will defend to the death his right to say it!" He laughed at his own wit. "Many of his theories are similar to mine."

"Theories about here?"

"Naturally."

"Could you explain them to me?"

"It would take hours."

"Another time?"

He shook my hand. "I will explain why things are so bad," he said, "and why there are probably no solutions to our problems."

"Sounds bleak, Shu."

"I am an optimist," he agreed.

"Say hello to Li Wei," I said in the stairwell. "I hope we meet her soon."

He did not miss a beat. "She is coming on Wednesday," he said. Another Shu-ism: inviting guests to the apartment without mentioning it beforehand. Shu was always generous with our hospitality.

Dust was to Beijing what fog was to London. Microscopic granules of Gobi Desert swept down from Inner Mongolia, unfazed by the broad plains, barren hills, even the mythic prowess of the Great Wall, and visited the capital like a prophesy, darkening noon to dusk and blurring midnight into dawn. At one time, Beijingers subsisted on a diet of clotted yellow air, the preindustrial equivalent to today's factory-emission eye burn and hacking cough. Dust was evidence of an inhospitable natural world beyond the Great Wall that was capable of inveighing against civilization with inundations of raw desert that penetrated windows and doors without restraint. Tree-planting campaigns on the edge of the Gobi in the 1950s, however, designed to erect an extreme outer line of defense, proved effective, and the desert itself appeared to turn inward, not tamed so much as disinclined to venture south. Air remained dry—the city was built on an arid plain—and sparse rainfall continued to reduce playing fields to powder and grass to weeds, but the will of nature to harass had subsided. Our first year in Beijing passed with only the faintest storms. Graduating students from the provinces expected to depart the capital deprived of a single Gobi dust tale, while natives had to rummage among memories to come up with a worthy tempest.

Until, that is, the morning after Shu Sheyu's visit, when the wind rose in increments and the sky sagged onto buildings. The effect was disconcerting, like being inside a collapsing tent. By early afternoon, the air was gray with swirling particles. Next, even stranger, calm returned—not a breath of wind, the light opaque—and the sky simply dissolved into earth and the earth into sky. The sun, meanwhile, glowered from a corner, engulfed in a widening ring of black. The air was now golden and tasted of baking soda. Sidewalks and pathways shimmied beneath the feet; benches were covered in dust. At four o'clock, the campus was deserted, all sports canceled, all activities moved indoors.

I decided to take a walk. In the silence, I charted my own labored breathing and worked to lighten my clunking footsteps over the pavement. Near the west gate I encountered a fellow pilgrim. Though barely ten meters away, the figure was indistinct, compelling me to rub my eyes on a jacket sleeve. The figure hailed me; it was Dean Shen. "Out for a reason?" he asked.

"I've never seen anything like this before," I answered.

He laughed, removed his glasses, scratched his forehead, jounced from foot to foot. The dean was a notorious bundle of nerves. "Maybe a big storm," he offered. "Like years ago. You should stay inside."

"So should you."

"Me?" he said in surprise.

"Why not you?"

"For me it's too late!" Dean Shen replied mysteriously.

I passed through the west gate into the alley where shops normally did brisk business at this hour and free-market vendors, lining both sides of the lane, hawked fruits and vegetables, slabs of meat, sacks of peanuts, bins of bean curd, barrels of flopping fish, woks, pots, shoe repairs, even stacks of well-handled girlie magazines. Now the alley was empty, the vendors vanished. A brief stroll brought me to the rear entrance of our neighbor college, an institute of commerce, and I walked past an unmanned guardhouse onto the campus. An eighteen-story apartment tower, the tallest building in the district, seemed to sway as I passed beneath it. Invisible under the sidewalk dust was the chalk mark from last October outlining where a graduate student had avoided arrest for sedition by jumping off the tower's top floor. Arrests, on-campus interrogations, students lifted from classes and not seen again were common over here, and the school administration had fared less well than ours at protecting its own. The institute had only two foreigners, both exotic Asian-Soviets, and my strolls had typically turned heads and garnered smiles. Today, though, I moved through a world of my own imagining: boarded classrooms, vacant fields, apartment blocks of flapping curtains and broken windows.

Reaching the front gate, on the main road into the city, I exited again—the man in the guardhouse stared blankly at my huffing apparition—and continued a few paces to where the entrance met the outer wall of a row of shops. The first building was a charred hole, but the second still functioned as a store for obscure machine parts. Below a shop window was a hieroglyph that had once fascinated the neighborhood but now merited only a passing glance. The hieroglyph consisted of gouges made by bullets that had missed their fleshy targets and then failed to penetrate concrete. The gouges were finger-sized, smooth and deep. Where once these bullet holes had constituted a minor sideshow in a dazzling display of urban warfare, they were now all that remained. I had begun to visit the site every so often to squat before the wall and explore the incisions, map their terrains. For this I drew stares and the occasional reproach from locals, who interpreted my action as veiled protest or criticism of apathy and forgetfulness. It was neither. The impulse was private and the purpose, if I could have identified it, was meditative.

Twilight had fallen by the time I followed the main road a kilometer back to our campus. The sky had cleared miraculously an hour before and the air no longer gagged. Narrowly avoiding a major storm had buoyed the community; the paths were once more bustling, children on bicycles weaving between packs of chattering adults, many of whom wore surgeons' masks or held handkerchiefs over their mouths. Relief was palpable, almost giddy. I was still having trouble breathing and hurried to the apartment to cough up yellow phlegm and convalesce a throat that would feel the next morning as if it had been roughed with sandpaper.

7

TEX-MEX

I t was the eve of Qingming Festival, and our turn to cook a Western meal. No East-West hybrids tonight, we vowed, no crossover dishes whose blandness, exacerbated by a lack of ingredients, would allow guests to satisfy a mild longing for international cuisine while inadvertently confirming their faith in their own gastronomic superiority. No spaghetti ("Marco Polo brought spaghetti to the West"), no fried chicken ("Emperors in the Tang Dynasty ate this dish") and no dumplings ("*Jiao zi* are tastier"): that was one fire Mary and I refused to feed. What we had in mind were tortillas. "A Mexican dish," I explained at the door. "Mexican ingredients with American influences, especially from the Southwest. They call the cuisine Tex-Mex. Not fancy—basic food."

"Basic American food?" Shu Sheyu asked.

"Basic food," I answered. "Both American and Mexican, I guess. A little of both. Everyone eats tortillas."

"In Mexico?"

"Right."

"And in Texas?"

"Sure."

"But you are from Toronto," he pointed out. "Shouldn't we have Canadian food?"

"Everyone loves tortillas."

"In Toronto also?"

"It's hard to explain ..."

Shu humphed and helped himself to the bowl of walnuts on the table. His appearance without the feminist track-and-field star was hardly surprising; Shu rarely showed up when, or with whom, he said he would. Instead of Li Wei, we said hello to Sun Zhimo, an affable math teacher from Shaanxi province with solid English comprehension but limited oral skills. Sun and I played basketball together most afternoons; I spoke with him in my language and he replied in his own, a linguistic detente that suited us both. Sun Zhimo was a slim twenty-nine-year-old, an ardent reader of contemporary literature and lover of American jazz. On the court, he liked to scat Charlie Parker or Duke Ellington melodies, syncopating his dribble and thrashing an imaginary cymbal—*da-da-da-da, bam! bam!*—after scoring a basket. Though I knew almost nothing about jazz, I still managed to lose my concentration long enough for Sun to make a steal, leading to an easy lay-up. His smile would be broad. "'Night in Tunisia,' Charlie," he would whisper in his phonetic English. "*Da-da-da-da, bam! bam!*"

Our other guests included Mary's closest friend, Zhang Naiying, and Zhao Zhenkai. Naiying, a Beijinger who had studied at the college a few years before and was now the English department's bright light, was an attractive woman with enormous eyes and a frank, friendly smile. Her face kept no secrets; when sad she looked sad, when happy she lit up like a flattered diva. Naiying was adored by her students, popular with men and remained in favor with the department despite a series of openly rebellious actions. The first was her participation in the demonstrations, and it was followed by incessant efforts to gain entrance into an American or Canadian university, and several paid absences during the winter to act as tour guide to groups of Taiwanese. Things came to a head in the final week in March when she actually quit the institute, a decision that Dean Shen sidestepped by labeling her absence an extended sick leave to allow her to keep her room, pay and food tickets. The dean's desperation to mollify Naiying was understandable; she was among his finest teachers on a list riddled with the missing, the vanished, the temporarily-on-leave-since-the-mid-1980s, the studying-abroad-but-delayed-in-returning. Simply to *have* a good teacher within arm's reach was incentive enough for Dean Shen to initiate a keep-Zhang campaign. Naiyang's favored status was attributed as well to the fact that she was a Party member in good, or at least reasonable, or "not-too-bad" standing.

Zhao Zhenkai, another of our guests, was also one of the department's aces. But Zhao, a flawless English speaker who had spent three years working in the embassy in London, was even more marginal than Naiying; he'd chosen to be designated a "temporary worker" until something better came along. That meant he received no residency card, no food tickets, no accommodation (he was staying in the room of a teacher-ghost), all of which suited him fine. In addition to awaiting word about scholarships from several British universities, Zhao was entertaining offers from the international business community in Beijing—hotels, banks, airlines. Unhampered by the usual five-year contract, breakable only with permission from the dean, Zhao Zhenkai was considered lucky.

Naiying was telling us about her recent national tour with a group of Australian doctors. The thrill of using her English skills, and the relief of not having to deal with the chauvinistic Taiwanese, had her in fine spirits. "We made jokes the whole time," she said. "Like, 'Welcome to the last socialist paradise on earth.' Also, 'Come visit our wonderful People's Republic before the people are all killed.'"

"The government should organize a tourism campaign for Eastern Europeans who miss socialism," Zhao said. "They could make big money selling nostalgia. 'Come see how it used to be in your country!'"

"Hungarians who enjoyed the Soviet invasion in 1956 could visit the museum and admire the tanks," I said. "Also Czechs who liked the 1968 version."

Tanks and artillery used on June 4 were now on display in a Beijing museum, in celebration of the crushing of the counterrevolutionary rebellion. Business at the exhibit was brisk, especially with troops of schoolchildren bound together with rope to discourage them from straying.

Even Shu, normally slow off the mark in English, managed a little black humor. "They should feature a new event at the Asian Games in September," he said. "Tanks could chase students around a field and try to run them over."

"Each school could present a team," Zhao added. "Beijing University against the 28th Army. Qinghua University against the 34th Army. I wonder who we would play?"

Zhao's comments were bitter, but not out of step with the mood of the others. It was telltale that such a mood would surface so quickly, even before alcohol was served. Tracking despair and gauging depression had become an integral part of our social interactions. People dropped by for a visit and wound up confessing their humiliation and confusion, their longing to flee, desire to withdraw, states of emptiness and sorrow and, more than once, their indifference to life. These soliloquies—talking to a foreigner was considered akin to talking to oneself—were delivered without prompting and typically overwhelmed all present until the room was filled with brooding silence.

Unwilling to let the gloom settle tonight, I slipped on the Cui Jian cassette and, after consulting Mary, skipped the preliminaries and got down to business. "Let me explain how this works," I said, bringing out plates of food. "Everyone pay attention."

The table was soon littered with a bewildering selection of dishes. Setbacks in shopping had forced repeated reinterpretations of Tex-Mex cuisine, with not altogether pleasing results. Homemade tortillas were the highlight, and the diced chicken sauteed in a wok was decent. Finding no kidney beans, we soaked a pot of tiny red pellets overnight and then boiled, baked and mashed them into a pulp that passed, barely, as refried beans. A sticky bland cheese was grated, tomatoes were chopped, and we substituted tender local cabbage for lettuce. Bottles of chili sauce from Sichuan were cooled with more tomatoes, producing a sweet but workable salsa, and at the last minute, losing artistic control, I woked up a mess of homefried potatoes, which had nothing to do with the theme. The meal was, in short, a mess.

"It looks delicious," Naiying offered.

Shu, already devouring a second helping, mumbled something—likely a critique—and refilled his beer glass. Zhao Zhenkai's years abroad had accustomed him to bizarre eating rituals, and he adjusted his glasses, rolled his sleeves and tucked in. Sun Zhimo, the math teacher, was having second thoughts, but he was also starved, a good sport, and shared with me the frank thought that he couldn't imagine the food would kill him. Receiving my assurances, Sun proceeded to heap unnatural quantities of each ingredient atop his tortilla. Unable to fold it, he then took up his knife and fork and sawed. Naiying rarely touched food, and Mary and I were as yet too anxious to eat. But the slipping and sliding that accompanied novice tortilla dining was having its desired effect; our guests were laughing, at themselves, but mostly at our cooking.

"That must be the new version of Cui Jian," Zhao said, referring to the music. "I've never heard the whole tape before."

"Is it better than the original mix?"

"More professional." He shrugged. "More Western."

Cui Jian's only recording to date, done in a local studio, had recently been remixed professionally. The new Cui Jian was sharp and crisp, his gravelly voice sounding more than ever like the balladeering of a solitary herdsman. What made Cui's music unique, arguably the most original cultural icon of the late 1980s, was its unselfconsciousness. Rock, reggae, techno-pop, even flickers of jazz informed a sophisticated sensibility that had been nurtured on folk and classical music traditions. Cui blended disparate, even potentially dissonant musical sources in the way young children of different races play in schoolyards. His anthem, the "Blowin' in the Wind" of our students' generation, was the ballad "Yi Wu Shuo You" ("I Am Nothing"). Not only did everyone know the lyrics by heart, but the melody, or the tune within the melody, was virtually a cradle song. "I Am Nothing" was unquestionably Cui's own composition. Several times, though, I heard snatches of a similar melodic line in recordings of Ming dynasty court and dance music. Detractors of Cui's rock and roll attitudes (the remix of "I Am Nothing" burst into a double-time coda fueled by a blistering guitar solo) and haughty Western ways kept stumbling over the paradox of musical congruence. Not the sound but *inside* the sound, not the notes but *below* the notes; there his music was eminently hummable and he remained, indisputably, a native son.

Cui Jian and his band, currently composed of a Japanese guitarist and three Beijingers, had been dodging censorship since their legendary early gigs in embassies and joint-venture hotels in 1986–87. Postmassacre activities had included an aborted tour of the south, furtive and frequently canceled performances in bars in the Sanlitun district of Beijing (word would be leaked only on the morning of the show, allowing club owners to plead ignorance if harassed by the PSB) and, somewhat surprisingly, an appearance at an official concert in February to raise money for the Asian Games. Cui's performance that night had captured the attention of the international press. A *Herald-Tribune* article on the crackdown against artists a few days later featured a photo of Cui playing his trumpet while blindfolded. The symbolism appeared unambiguous, especially before a crowd littered with government cadres. For weeks afterward I waited for friends to mention Cui's provocative act. Finally, I offered the photo to our dinner guests.

"Did any of you hear about this?" I asked.

"Cui is such a show-off!" Zhao chuckled.

"I was at the concert," Shu said.

"What was it like?"

"Noisy," he replied, stuffing a fourth tortilla.

"What about when Cui put on the blindfold. Did the audience react?"

"It is easy to play the trumpet with a blindfold," Shu said. "Only three fingers are needed."

Naiying examined the newspaper article. She was a rarity: an avowed non-Cui Jian fan.

"Cui likes to do strange things," she said. "He often wears army clothes during his concerts and marches around the stage like a soldier. Probably he learned these tricks from Western singers."

"The paper thinks it was a protest," I said.

"What was?"

"Wearing a blindfold."

"A protest against what?" Naiying asked.

"Well ..." I said, at a loss where to begin.

"The government, you mean?" Zhao interjected. "The international press believes that Cui wore the blindfold to show his disrespect for Deng Xiaoping?"

"Something like that."

He laughed. "People here didn't interpret it that way. We just think Cui is being a show-off. He is a little conceited, you know, especially since the American record company gave him a contract."

For years it had been rumored that a major American label was interested in recording Cui Jian. Though the contract had never materialized, and Cui had been outside the country only briefly, his apparent good fortune displeased many.

"It is said that he has many hoodlum friends," Naiying offered. "Men who ride motorcycles and help him at his concerts."

I didn't see the connection.

"They are rough and violent," she explained. "Hooligans and criminals—*liu mang*. Why sould Cui Jian be seen with these people?"

Liu mang: hooligans, punks, nonconformists, nihilists. A legacy of the Cultural Revolution, this class of urban youth tended to be ill-educated and underemployed, basically bored, shiftless kids who had little time for their parents and no time for the political ideology that had rendered that generation so timid and servile. Beijing's underworld was presumed to be *liu mang* controlled.

"Cui is no longer popular with students," Naiying concluded, a comment at odds with the fact that she had been silently mouthing the lyrics to his songs. "Maybe now he will become a star in America."

Sun Zhimo had put down his utensils to read the article, frowning at words he did not recognize. He lowered the *Herald-Tribune*. "Yes," he said.

We waited.

"Cui Jian," he said. "This photo, the—" He indicated the blindfold. "It is *kangyi*."

Protest.

"The—" Sun continued, again pointing to the blindfold. "Is us. Our *yanjing*."

"Eyes," I said.

"Yes. Our eyes."

The table fell silent.

"Having trouble, Sun?" I said quickly. Sun Zhimo's difficulties at cutting his first tortilla had compelled a new strategy. After deliberation, the second tortilla was hacked into four quarters *before* any toppings were applied.

Shu Sheyu examined his friend's work. "Four Modernizations," he said.

Sun covered the first wedge in chicken and tomato. "Industry," he announced.

"Looks tasty," Naiying said.

Shu doused a second quarter in beans and sauce. "Agriculture," he explained. Picking up Sun's tortilla, he gobbled it whole. "My favorite." Shu laughed so hard he nearly choked. Others laughed as well.

"I'll try Science and Technology," Zhao Zhenkai said. Receiving the plate, he smothered his wedge in potatoes, cheese and beans. That left only one of the Party's "Four Modernizations;" everyone waited for someone else to make an offer. At last Sun himself buried the remaining tortilla quarter in chicken, beans, potatoes, cheese, cabbage and tomato, with bloody blotches of sauce on top. "My father was in the army," he said in his own language. "He fought for liberation."

Sun ate National Defense.

Levity had been restored to the evening. Immediately, some idiot went and ruined it. "Where's the Fifth Modernization?" I asked.

The phrase belonged to counterrevolutionary Wei Jingsheng. It referred to his famous "Fifth Modernization" of democracy and human rights. Wei had written: "Democracy, freedom and happiness are the only goals of modernization. Without this Fifth Modernization, the four others are nothing more than a newfangled lie."

"He's in Qinghai," Shu said reluctantly, referring to the remote province where Wei Jingsheng was believed to be incarcerated. Though possibly the freest person I knew in Beijing, even Shu Sheyu winced before the spectre of Wei Jingsheng and his imprisonment. ("I was too young when it happened," he once explained.) He pretended otherwise, but Shu's morose decapitation of a beer bottle, performed in defiance of Mary's request that he spare us the trick, chronicled better than any words his frustration. He even rotated the cap in his mouth and gnawed on it, smiling like a naughty child.

More beer was poured, and the conversation deteriorated into a bitching session. Astrophysicist Fang Lizhi, still receiving sanctuary with his wife in the American embassy a half hour's bicycle ride from our dormitory, was dispensed with easily; Fang's wholesale dismissal of socialism and embrace of democracy was far too extreme for most intellectuals, even those able to recognize the playfulness and devil's advocacy of his positions. Wu'er Kaixi also got slammed; magazine photos were examined of Wu'er aboard the *Goddess of Democracy*, a ship headed for Taiwan as a French-supported publicity stunt to broadcast antigovernment radio messages, and close attention was paid to the young dissident's jowly cheeks and expensive suit. Student activist Chai Ling, still missing following the crackdown, also came under fire from our guests.

Zhang Naiying finally took a few bites of food, only to interrupt her cold dinner to tell us the story of popular leader Wang Dan's arrest in July. What was interesting about Naiying's tale was not that Wang was arrested after meeting a Taiwanese reporter, but that he had already fled Beijing once, returned, and was in the process of orchestrating his own exile when the police stumbled upon him. Wang's sensible desire to escape the country was oddly immaterial to the legend of a man awaiting his fate with stoic resignation, at peace with himself and at home among his followers. Wang Dan *was* a courageous and defiant man. But was he the martyr of Naiying's story? As a hero, he suited the population better than the leaders-in-exile in France or the United States simply because he was in a position exactly like that of those at home: silent, suffering, incarcerated. "Wang was the most intelligent student leader," Naiying said. "He was also the most respected by Beijingers. We place great hope in Wang Dan."

"He is more acceptable to intellectuals than the others," Zhao explained. "Wang is very bright and articulate. Also he comes from a good family and avoided the foreign press during the student movement."

"He didn't like to have his picture taken," Naiying said.

"Professors at Beida say he was their best student," Shu added, using the abbreviation for Beijing University. "Except that he never had time to go to classes."

"We place great hope in Wang Dan," Naiying repeated.

Before people left, I called attention to our mystery sheet of calligraphy, now hanging on the wall across from the couch.

"Is this the writing on the wall?" Zhao wondered, pleased with himself.

"Maybe," I said. "Only no one can read it."

"It's peculiar," he agreed.

"Ancient," Naiying offered. "Perhaps more than one thousand years old."

Claiming he could decipher all varieties of calligraphy, Shu crossed the room to examine the sheet. He considered the ideographs, squinting furiously.

"Well?" I said.

"I'm drunk," Shu answered. "I'm going home."

"What about you, Sun?"

Sun Zhimo thrashed his imaginary cymbal. *"Da-da-da-da, bam! bam!"* he said. "Like Shu."

"Drunk?"

"Maybe. Also ..." He reverted to his native tongue. "I teach at eight o'clock tomorrow morning," he said.

"We all teach tomorrow," Shu said. "Departments were told by the administration that no teacher will be allowed to be absent on Qing-ming Festival."

"The security guards will try to prevent anyone from leaving campus," Naiying explained. "If you insist on going outside, they copy down your identification number."

"And ...?"

"Trouble," she said.

"Will there be trouble tomorrow?" I asked.

"On campus?"

"In Beijing."

"Perhaps," Naiying said.

"Perhaps not," Zhao amended.

"I will make trouble by starting my class with a minute of silence for the victims of the Tiananmen massacre," Shu announced. "Then I will leave flowers on an empty desk."

At the door, Naiying said something to Shu. Her tone was low and hard, but he only shrugged. "I don't care," he said in English. He offered a song:

"Wo ceng jing wen ge bu xiu
Ni he shi gen wo zou
Ke ni que zong shi xiao wo
Yi wu shuo you"

("I've asked you so many times
When will you accompany me
But all you do is laugh,
And tell me I am nothing")

"Zhou Shuren is friends with Cui Jian," Zhao said, aware that we knew Zhou. "At least he claims he is. He has many connections with those kinds of people."

"*Liu mang?*" I asked.

"Zhou doesn't like teachers," Naiying said.

"But Dean Shen likes him," Zhao added without explanation.

"Watch your step, Shu," I called in the landing. "Maybe Naiying should take your arm."

"I am nothing," Shu laughed.

"You are drunk!" his friend corrected.

Five minutes later, Zhou Shuren called from the reception desk downstairs. It was nearly curfew, and the night porter rarely allowed guests in so late. But Zhou had good relations with the security personnel, and came and went with the impunity normally reserved for administration officials and Westerners. He had to speak with us, he apologized over the phone, and proceeded to climb the stairs to our floor with vigor if not accuracy, slipping twice. Zhou headed for the couch and Shu Sheyu's half-finished bottle. I explained the mess. "We had guests," I said.

"I know," he answered. "The old man at the desk asked me to provide the names of everyone who ate dinner here. Only one teacher signed in, Zhao Zhenkai."

"Did you inform on us, Zhou?"

"Of course. I said that Bruce Springsteen, Mick Jagger, Bono and Madonna had dinner in your apartment tonight."

Zhou performed his own beer trick, inverting the bottle into the glass without incident. He gazed intently at the curtains, as if expecting someone to emerge from behind them. "I have to ask you about Atlantic City," he said.

"Sure."

"I am going away tomorrow. A journey, you see. A journey of discovery and recovery. I need your help."

"What can we do?"

"There is a story," Zhou said, gulping his beer, "about a monk who is being pursued by the soldiers of a dictator who has decreed that all freethinkers and wise men must die. The monk is also being chased by the assassins of a second dictator, who is in competition with the first." He paused to refill his glass. "So the man is running from one army when he comes to a cliff. Having no choice, he begins to climb down the face. He looks up and sees the assassins he is fleeing. He looks down, however, and sees more soldiers, from the other dictator. Above is death; below is death also. But the monk is looking straight ahead. What does he spy before his eyes?" Zhou asked rhetorically. "A flower, his favorite food. 'Ah,' the monk says, plucking the flower and eating it. 'Life is sweet.'"

I nodded, expecting more. But the tale was over. Sensing my confusion, Zhou elaborated. "The past is shit, you see. The future is shit also. Only the present can be like a flower—sweet to smell, tasty to eat." He demonstrated by plucking an imaginary flower from the air, inhaling its perfume, then placing the stem between his teeth.

"Live for the moment?" I said.

"That's right."

"Where are you going?"

"I have a sick brother," Zhou said.

"I'm sorry."

"Have I told you about the time I died in Tibet?"

"I don't think so."

"Do you have more beer?"

Mary brought another bottle.

"I was with a crew climbing to the base camp of Mount Everest. There was no air, you see, and I had been sick already for a week. Several times during the morning I stopped and announced that I could not go on. My body was a cramped muscle and I suffered from dizziness, like when very drunk. The boss got angry with me and said I should just lie down in the snow and die. Which I did," Zhou said, smiling meditatively. "I collapsed and let the snow build a coffin for my body. Soon I stopped being cold, and though the wind swirled snow above where I lay, it didn't sting my skin any longer. The sky moved like a film and all around was white, white, white, as in heaven. But I lay still, becoming white also as the snow piled up, listening to my own breathing—" Zhou closed his eyes and drew several deep breaths to summon the image "—and feeling my eyes rotate in their sockets."

"How long did you lie there?" I asked.

"Until I died. It was so beautiful, so clean, only my body and the moving blue sky and the white, white, white, that I didn't care what happened. I was eating the flower, you see, eating the sweet flower and not worrying about the assassins above and below."

"Did they really abandon you in the snow?" Mary said.

"For a while I watched the expedition advance along the slope of the mountain, tiny specks of dirt against a white wall. Who cared? They were nothing, and I was nothing too."

"So you died," I summarized.

"That's right."

"How did it feel?"

"Better than this," Zhou answered. "At one moment, I floated above my coffin and looked down at the body inside it. 'Not interesting,' I decided, and then floated higher and higher into the blue, only the blue above and the white below, pure colors, you see, and no people, absolutely *no* people, which made it like a sweet, sweet flower."

Zhou drank. I pondered. "Sounds like a dream," I finally said.

"It was," he agreed. "Or else this is. Maybe *I* am."

"A dream?"

"That is what was best about Tibet," he said. "There were no people to keep telling me what was a dream and what was not a dream. I *hate* it when people tell me this."

The gurgle of the telephone startled us. The night porter was about to chain the doors.

"Can I borrow some tapes for my trip?" he asked. "Just like last year."

"You remember that night?"

"I remember last year," he replied. "Even though it was only a dream." He crossed to the cabinet and ran a finger over the row of cassettes, selecting three.

"Are you going to visit your brother?"

"I am stupid," Zhou informed us. "The sickness is mental. Mental illness."

"I'm sorry," Mary offered.

"Mental illness in all my family."

"Where does your brother live?"

He didn't answer.

"Will you be gone for long?"

"Yes, no," he said.

I escorted Zhou down the stairs. The porter, a friendly old man, stood at the door in his pajamas, ready to latch the handles with a chain. Zhou stopped to burp.

"You're leaving tomorrow?" I said. "On Qingming?"

"Where's Atlantic City again?" he asked.

I hesitated. "It's in Shandong province," I answered.

"Good. Not too far away."

Zhou left, and the door was chained. Our building, tucked into a corner of the campus, featured a glassed-in corridor that ran parallel to the path leading visitors back to the main thoroughfares. I followed Zhou's outline the length of the building, rustling the curtains with my hand to show him that I, or someone, was within, only hidden. He did speak, but his words were inaudible. Then the corridor ended with another locked door, and I lost Zhou completely.

PART II

TIANANMEN

TIANANMEN

I t is certainly hard to live in this world. To "lack wordly wisdom" is not good, but neither is it good to have "too much worldly wisdom." Apparently worldly wisdom is like revolution. "A revolution is needed but it should not be too radical." You need some worldly wisdom, but not too much.

Once a thing is described, it has its limitations and its quintessence is lost for good. So to talk of the "quintessence of worldly wisdom" is a contradiction in terms. The truth of the quintessence lies in deeds not words; yet just by saying "deeds not words" I have let slip the Truth again, and am further from the quintessence.*

April 15, 1989, was a dusty Saturday at the heart of a dusty month. The sky was a stinging blue and the heavy air trapped the heat. Though summer was still far off, the campus had sunk into a torpor. Qingming Festival had passed without incident ten days before: routine mourning for routine deaths. April would blur into May and May would dissolve into June, when there would be final exams, farewell parties, expulsion notices in the dormitories, tickets out of the capital.

*All italicized citations in this chapter are from the essays of Lu Xun (1881–1936), China's greatest modern writer. Lu's work remains as relevant today as during his own lifetime.

No one could study. No one could think. Temperatures soared, and for the fourteenth consecutive day rain refused to fall.

The *China Daily*, our morning dose of translated propaganda, opened its April 15 edition with the headline "Premier Li says China politically stable." The prime minister, intent on quelling rumors of a rift with General Secretary Zhao Ziyang, explained that "on the whole" he and Zhao "cooperated very well, though they were not entirely of the same views."

There was more news that weekend. Though not announced until Monday, the death of Hu Yaobang was a whisper on campus by Saturday evening and a roar before Sunday noon. Hu, the disgraced former general secretary, had been dismissed in 1987 in part because of his lackadaisical crackdown on the *last* student movement. Word had it that he had suffered a heart attack during an argument with Li Peng over the state of higher education. Allowed to retain his politbureau seat to save face, a frustrated Hu Yaobang had arrived at a meeting armed with a paper on education that he insisted on reading. The frail mandarin launched into a passionate defense of universities, with emphasis on the woeful status of teachers and/or students (depending on who was telling the tale), only to be felled by a weary heart. Hu died fighting for education. Hu died with the word "reform" on his lips. So, at least, claimed the rumors.

I asked a fourth-year student about Hu Yaobang on Monday.

"He died for us," the student intoned. "For intellectuals."

"Why did he do that?" I wondered.

"To help our cause," the boy answered.

"What cause?"

"The cause of intellectuals," he said. "Us. Our problems."

"What is your cause?" I pressed.

"The same as everyone else's?" the student said uneasily.

"The cause that Hu died for?" I proposed.

"That's it!" he agreed.

Shu Sheyu was more helpful. I met him at the bulletin board across from the cafeteria, a wall of rain-smeared, sun-bleached sheets of rice paper that vied for the attention of campus dwellers.

The board was normally littered with administration notices, medical clinic business and announcements of activities. It rarely drew a crowd, except when a disgruntled citizen sneaked out after curfew to post an anonymous complaint. National affairs were never mentioned directly in the posters, and decorum excluded graffiti on what constituted, by default, the local wire service. But by late in the day on April 17 a few mild salvos had been fired—"Hu, we will miss you" and "Yaobang, you died too soon"—and dozens of students were milling about the sidewalk excitedly. Shu translated the slogans for me.

"People seem genuinely affected by Hu's death," I said.

"He was an ally," Shu replied. "We have very few."

"Was Hu involved in education reform?"

He grinned at my naiveté. "He was a leader," Shu said. "Involved in leading." We were silent for a moment. "Hu Yaobang was decent," he continued. "Among high officials only Hu and Zhao Ziyang understood the changes that are needed to help the country. Also, they tried to protect intellectuals from persecution. Now the reformers have lost. Li Peng and the old men ..." He stopped. "Deng," he clarified, his smile tightening. "Always Deng. Only Deng."

"But I thought Hu was Deng's protégé?" I said. "Why did he dismiss him two years ago?"

Shu shrugged. "Politics," he said. "Always politics. Only politics."

Shu related a favorite anecdote about Hu Yaobang. During a controversial state visit to Japan in 1986 (Japanese rewriting of the events of World War II was causing a furor in China at the time), the general secretary was treated to a song and dance performance by three thousand youths. Impressed by their discipline and talents, and determined to show off the equal skills of Chinese children, Hu spontaneously invited the Japanese brood on an all-expenses-paid trip to the People's Republic. His largesse infuriated colleagues, but for Shu the gesture was endearing.

"Hu acted oddly sometimes and made strange comments," he explained. "He seemed normal to us."

"Was Hu Yaobang one of you?" I asked.

"Of course not," Shu answered. "He was a leader."

On the way to his dormitory, Shu also mentioned that he had just got off the phone with a friend at Beijing University. Things were happening at Beida. Remarkable things. Worrisome things.

Zhou Shuren, whom I ran into on Wednesday evening, was even more blunt. Actually, it was Zhou who ran into me, on his bicycle, along the path near the south gate. Spotting a friendly face, Zhou tried to wave, lost control and lurched. I sidestepped the bike, grabbed the handlebars. Zhou was just returning from a night out in the city, a night out on Tiananmen Square. Students and faculty from various Beijing schools had marched on Monday in memory of Hu Yaobang. Wreaths had appeared on Tiananmen the next day, along with banners and posters, and a small nocturnal sit-in was organized before the Great Hall of the People on the west side of the square. Happily, according to the official press, the protests were not protests and the protesters were actually patriotic citizens expressing their grief at the untimely death of a venerable Party member.

Zhou was one such patriot. "When people say Hu," he offered, "I say 'Who?' When they say Yaobang, I say *bu yao* [don't want]."

I needed a minute to take in his bilingual puns. "Wasn't Hu a friend to intellectuals?" I asked.

"Who?" Zhou said. Then, more seriously, "Did you know that Hu Yaobang once claimed that an artist should be allowed only 20 percent 'dark' material in his work? The other 80 percent must be devoted to the positive sides of socialism! Some friend," he concluded.

"Then why mourn his death?"

"Why not?" Zhou answered.

"Are you protesting, Zhou?"

"That's right," he agreed.

"Against what?"

"Everything,"

"Elvis Presley?" I said.

"That's right," he agreed again. "I am protesting against the death of Elvis Presley."

I elaborated. "There is a famous story about when Elvis Presley was young and had a bad attitude. A journalist asked him, 'What are you protesting about?' Elvis replied, 'What d'ya got?'"

"What d'ya got?" Zhou repeated, savoring the American diction.

"But then Elvis was drafted into the army," I added, completing an unhappy thought. "Things were different afterward."

Zhou climbed back onto his bicycle. "Don't worry," he said. "I won't join the army. I hate guns. Also, the uniforms are ugly, and the hats look stupid."

Expressions of grief rose out of Beijing all that week. Spearheaded by students from the major universties, the vigils on Tiananmen Square grew slowly in size and rapidly in importance. On Thursday, April 20, mourners, including a few from our school, carried a six-meter-high portrait of Hu Yaobang and a seven-point petition that they hoped to present to Party leaders before the gates of Zhongnan-hai, the Party leadership compound, a kilometer west of the square. Demands ranged from the disclosure of politicans' salaries and an end to bureaucratic corruption to freedom of the press and a separation of the judiciary from the Party. Official response was silence, though offense was taken at the impropriety of such action when Hu's state funeral was still two days off.

The funeral was equally improper. Inside the Great Hall of the People, the cabal that had schemed to depose Hu Yaobang mourned lugubriously over the corpse, while demonstrators entered the square before police could cordon it off, to wave banners and shout slogans. Though several banners mentioned the dead mandarin, most protesters stepped gingerly over Hu Yaobang's body to battle other shadows: "Down with Dictatorship," "Down with Bureaucracy" and "Long Live Democracy." Students also knelt on the steps of the Great Hall in an act of supplication designed to shame leaders into initiating a dialogue with them. None did.

Though all this happened long ago, those who hanker for the past need not feel pessimistic. To all appearances there is still peace, for though there are often wars, droughts, and floods, have you ever heard anyone raise his voice in protest?

Our campus reacted slowly to the activity. Not until Sunday did our bulletin board posters approach the fervor of those displayed on the square. Friends and students, aware that the demonstrations were the work of the "big" schools, the traditional authors of unrest, admitted to feeling timid, as if to express ardor for the movement at this stage would be presumptuous, a challenge to the hierarchy of iconoclasm. Most appeared content to wait for a formal marching invitation from their cohorts across the city. Among acquaintances, only Zhou Shuren was primed for the fray. He whizzed past me on his bicycle Sunday afternoon, headed for the open road.

"Where are you going, Zhou?" I asked.

"Tiananmen Square," he answered.

"What are you rebelling against?"

"What d'ya got?" he replied.

The general invitation to protest arrived that same evening. The offer came not from Beida or Qinghua University, but from the institute next door. It took the form of a friendly raid on the men's dormitory, designed to goad our undergraduates into action. Hurrahs arced through the night air, rousing sleepers, and a posse went on to the foreign students' dormitory shouting "Come out!, Come out!" A rally was held, followed by a march peculiar in both its parameters—all paths led to locked gates—and its timing: a nighttime assault on downtown Beijing risked attracting little attention. Nevertheless, activists declared the event a success, settled on a plan and crawled back through crumbling walls and open windows for a few hours' sleep.

Next morning, students at our college joined those across the city in boycotting classes. Though a few straggled in, heads bowed in shame, most remained in their dormitories or slipped off campus to avoid the ensuing flurry of denunciations, visits from department heads and the depressing specter of class monitors, who were held responsible for the insubordination, rushing about begging friends to abandon the madness. Students insisted that their monitors vote on the boycott, and several of the smaller departments made the protest official. Monitors in the powerful English department, however, toed the line; the walkout was denounced. Still, classrooms remained largely empty, and Mary and I, like many foreign teachers, avoided charges of collusion by turning up at the appointed hour, surveying the rows of empty desks and declaring to those present that ill health or scheduling conflicts or the alluring sunshine had forced a postponement. Class was then dismissed, though all were welcome to chat over a yogurt in the cafeteria.

I had a problem with my graduate seminar. To be exact, I had a problem with Li Feigan. Li insisted that the seminar continue, that our discussions provide him with a forum to reflect equally on the obduracy of the government and the credulity of the students. He had no time for my argument that, personal opinions aside, the boycott should be respected simply because it was the will of the majority. I managed to shift the meetings to our apartment to cloak their existence and tried introducing harmless topics. It didn't work.

"The students are making a parade," Li offered in one seminar. "They are showing off their strong voices and witty slogans."

"Their demands are reasonable," I said. "Mostly things you have suggested in class."

"The government still will not listen," he replied, raising a hand to acknowledge my compliment.

"Suppose the protests keep growing?" I argued. "Suppose the boycott lasts until June?"

Li shrugged. "Classes are boring compared with a parade," he said. "In a parade you wave banners marked 'Long Live Reform!' and shout slogans like 'The People Are China!' These are more interesting activities for students than learning a foreign language or how to build a bridge."

"What about their demands?" I said. "An end to corruption and official profiteering. More democracy. More freedom of—"

"Demands are vague," Li interrupted. "Deng Xiaoping is real."

I took the bait. "Maybe demands are vague," I said, "but a hundred thousand people marching on Tiananmen Square—that's pretty real, isn't it?"

"The demonstrations are nothing," he repeated. "They are just a parade!"

The powers-that-be disagreed with Li Feigan's assessment. On Wednesday, April 26, after three more days of marches and boycotts and impossibly sunny skies, an editorial was published on the front page of the hardline Party newspaper, *People's Daily*, and conveniently translated, also on the front page, in the *China Daily*. The protesters were "reactionaries" whose purpose was to "poison people's minds, create national turmoil and sabotage the nation's political stability." A "clique" of students was involved in a planned conspiracy to "negate the leadership of the Party and the socialist system," and would, if it succeeded, reduce a promising China to a "turbulent and hopeless country."

The government would not let that happen.

Of course, a man wants to go on living. Even slaves, the lowest of the low, struggle to survive. But at least they know they are slaves. They endure hardships, burn with resentment and struggle to free themselves—sometimes they succeed in doing so. Even if defeated for a time and fettered again, they are simply slaves. But utterly damned are those who try to find "beauty" in slavery, praising and caressing it or being intoxicated by it, for they try to reconcile themselves and others to being slaves forever. This slight difference between slaves gives rise to the difference in society between peace and disturbances.

Students at our college awoke the morning of April 27 to loudspeaker blasts ordering them back to classes. The *People's Daily* editorial had rattled older faculty who remembered the Cultural Revolution well enough to flinch at the slightest hint that the masters in Zhongnanhai were displeased. Many men and women suffering the torments of divided loyalties and warring impulses retired to their rooms for the duration of the movement to agonize over the dilemma. A few, though, braver, stronger, more desperate, went public with their insecurities, becoming ambivalent and frequently unhelpful models for the students.

That Thursday, however, virtually the entire undergraduate population staged a sit-in outside the main classroom building. Organized by a few sophomores, the protest started when students arriving for classes were approached by friends, persuaded to support the action and invited to plunk themselves down on the curb. Besides the *People's Daily* editorial, there was little explanation why our school chose that morning to discover its political voice. Events began to occur spontaneously, almost inevitably, and for reasons that were often far from apparent. The sit-in itself was modest. No one chanted or shouted slurs, the singing of the "Internationale" was withheld until nighttime, and the majority of the students we chatted with confessed to nervousness, even doubt, about the wisdom of their actions. Again, as members of a small institute, the activists were content to follow: to seek advice from leaders at the major universities, to copy down memorable slogans and poems for local distribution, to listen to Chinese-language broadcasts on the BBC or "Voice of America" to hear what the movement's emerging spokesmen (notably Wang Dan and Wu'er Kaixi) were saying. Simply to be part of something blooming was adventure enough for most.

A number of undergraduates did slip away to enlist in the scholastic battalion that set out from the university corridor in northwest Beijing early in the afternoon. Ten thousand troops had been hustled into the city overnight. The student phalanx, in an astonishing show of defiance, confronted successive army barricades, and at each stage negotiated with soldiers to let them through, reaching Tiananmen Square late in the day. As an assertion of character, and the flexing of political muscle, the demonstration was unprecedented, an instant touchstone for future iconoclasts.

For those of us who tried to enter the square from the east side to witness the event, April 27 was less memorable. Chang'an Avenue was blocked by a wall of green uniforms, and these troops weren't budging. A crowd of several hundred milled before them, mostly commuters who lived across Beijing and now faced a half-hour detour around the Forbidden City. Worse than the congestion of office workers was the tangle of bicycles mired in an intersection already jammed with honking cars, bleating taxis, prams, pedicabs and the obligatory throng of locals engaged in the cheap, politically neutral pastime of gaping.

An old man, pressed against the human chain by the mob, was berating a teenage recruit for closing Tiananmen Square. The man brandished before the soldier a live chicken that he had to rush home to give to his wife to prepare for dinner. He had parked his bicycle in the shade of the Forbidden City, now off-limits. How would he get to it? The bird would die soon, or else cause mayhem on the bus. The old man demanded that he be allowed through the barricade to fetch his bike. Onlookers voiced agreement: a chicken dinner was no slight affair; chickens were expensive, and everyone knew that a fresh kill was more tasty. Still, the soldier refused. Incensed, the man muttered curses and waved the bird again. But then he announced to all assembled that he in no way blamed the army or the students for his ruined meal. The soldiers had their orders and the students were good kids, meant no harm. Though the old man wisely refrained from stating whom he did blame, it was clear enough, and his feelings reflected those of most bystanders. Beijingers, who might have been expected to be furious at the demonstrations, appeared to be taking matters in stride. Bilious editorials, threatening newscasts, troop reinforcements had made little visible impact on the crowds that gathered to watch, and sometimes to participate in, unlawful and potentially explosive protests. The mood of the crowd along Chang'an Avenue was free of the tensions and short tempers that often surfaced at large gatherings. Beijing was, at the best of times, not an especially friendly city. How to explain this transformation?

Zhang Naiying had a theory. She had marched on the square with friends from Beida and witnessed the support shown the students by locals, who'd offered food and drink and cheered as the activists passed each neighborhood. "Ordinary people like to enjoy the beautiful weather," Naiying explained to us. "They can eat ice cream and drink juice."

"That's it?" I said.

"Actually, it is quite a lot," she corrected, speaking with the authority of a native. "Beijingers have little opportunity to participate in civic events."

I was confused. "How is an illegal march organized by a movement that was denounced in all the newspapers a civic event?"

Naiying nodded patiently. "The government is not respected. They lack the support of the people."

"So are ordinary Beijingers defying the government?" I asked.

She smiled. "They are not so political," she said. "But the sun is bright and the sky is tall, like skies in other countries."

The next major "civic event" was held on May 4. The date was auspicious, being the seventieth anniversary of the 1919 student movement that had come to symbolize the revolutionary ideal in Chinese youth. Given the parallels—both were directed by students from Beida, both rallied on Tiananmen, both marched on the strongholds of their enemies—it was hardly a surprise that participants seemed subdued, taken aback by the length of shadows already cast across the square.

In the morning, a photogenic assembly of Communist Youth League recruits had gathered before the Monument to the People's Heroes to pledge oaths of allegiance to the Party and engage in some sluggish parading. Upon completion of these duties, the youths bolted from the scene with the dignity of pedestrians fleeing a car-bombed street. The new wave of marchers, also youthful, wore no school uniforms, pledged allegiance to no one, but were equally orderly and perfunctory, parading around Tiananmen with institute banners fluttering in the breeze. The liveliest spot was outside Zhongnanhai. Schools queued up for a position before the magnificent gate, defended by six unarmed soldiers, and then shouted slogans and hurled insults at the leaders, presumably cowering within. The crowd assembled for the spectacle proved discriminating judges, repeating striking phrases and applauding witty put-downs. Except for the ceremonial soldiers, the square and the surrounding streets were a free zone, clear of police and army. For one afternoon, the students had downtown Beijing to themselves, a gift from a compliant, or perhaps calculating, government. Though generous, the gift was also a test: the demonstration went off without a hitch but also without much passion, like a halftime show at a football game.

The hesitation was palpable. The boycott of classes was canceled the next day at our institute, and the more strident posters disappeared from the bulletin board. People debated whether to suspend the demonstrations. The May 4 rally had surpassed all expectations, broken all rules. The government had been thoroughly humiliated and needed time to respond. Their message had clearly been heard, and so far, not a single activist had been arrested or beaten. Wasn't that achievement enough?

Besides, final exams were barely a month away.

The pity is that the Chinese behave like wild beasts in front of sheep, but like sheep in front of wild beasts; so that even when we're acting like beasts, our country still appears cowardly ... In my opinion, to save China we need not develop any new qualities. If young people will reverse the traditional application of these two ancient attributes, that will be enough: When your opponent is a wild beast, act like a wild beast yourself; when he is a sheep, act like a sheep!

For then, no matter how cunning the devil may be, he will have to go back to his own hell.

I flagged down Zhou Shuren on the south road late on Saturday, May 13. Everything had changed in a week. An announcement had been made that morning that three hundred students were prepared to starve themselves to death if the leadership refused to commence a meaningful dialogue. In forty-eight hours, Soviet leader Mikhail Gorbachev would arrive in the capital to be greeted by the country's principal statesmen on the front steps of the Great Hall of the People, where protesters were now bunking down for the night. Dozens of foreign news crews were pouring into the country to cover the summit and were already snapping photos of headbanded youths. Furthermore, local media had recently confessed publicly to operating under censorship and the dictates of propaganda, and had promised more honest coverage. But the most fundamental of recent developments was an alteration in the tone of the movement. Insulted by government slurs, students were now demanding recognition that their activism was legitimate, insisting that they *could* love the country, even the Party, and still criticize both. The mood had turned confrontational, openly rebellious.

Mary and I were pondering this change when we met Zhou. We had just been on the square; he was heading downtown to disappear.

"I left a note on your door," he explained, "to say goodbye."

"Are things that serious?" I asked.

"Not serious. Just crazy."

"Is Zhao Ziyang winning the battle inside the Party?" I wondered earnestly.

"Zhao Yaobang or Hu Ziyang?" Zhou replied. "Maybe it is Li Xiaoping and Deng Peng who are in control. Maybe it is Mao Zedong or Ronald Reagan. I cannot be sure. I am too stupid to tell one old man from another."

"Where are you disappearing to?" I asked.

"Tiananmen Square."

"Are you going to join the hunger strike?"

"Maybe," Zhou said. "I don't know yet." He got back on his bike.

"What are you rebelling against, Zhou?" I said.

"What d'ya got?"

"Do you love your country?" I added, thinking of the students' desire to be recognized as patriots.

"I love my mother," Zhou replied. "And rock and roll, and beer and speaking English."

"And movies?"

"That's right," he agreed. "Especially movies with unhappy endings."

"Why those?" I asked.

"More realistic," he replied.

For once, cynicism seemed too easy. "What's happening in Beijing?" I pressed. "Isn't it different? Isn't it special?"

Zhou grinned. "Very special," he said. "Like a dream. I must be awake."

I was about to ask if he hadn't meant to say "asleep" when Zhou waved goodbye. He had no time to chat.

The week of Zhou Shuren's first disappearance, of Gorbachev's disastrous visit, the hunger strike, the largest demonstrations in the history of the People's Republic, of blistering sunshine and brutal downpours, of a free press reporting a freed will, of effervescent anarchy, miraculous calm, contagious high spirits, fitful optimism and, first and foremost, of no violence and remarkably little tension—that week began with an act of courage and ended with a declaration of cowardice. The streets around Tiananmen were filled with people, so we, like a million others, traveled in and out of Beijing on bicycles. Lanes were packed, the pace fast but never frantic, the mood all smiles and jokes and V-for-Victory signs. Nearer the square were the bike depots, unattended heaps of tangled metal. The vastness of Tiananmen—forty hectares of concrete—and the tank-friendly expanse of Chang'an Avenue, the artery across its northern flank, absorbed a quarter million visitors without fuss.

On Sunday, the hunger strikers occupied a patch of concrete at the base of the Monument to the People's Heroes. They lay on thin cotton mattresses and newspapers, sipping water and chatting, singing, dozing with hats over faces. Surrounding them were clusters of school contingents and haphazard squadrons of marchers, often fresh converts, who wove gingerly around the bodies to parade, then squatted in a randomly chosen spot that would constitute their territory for the week. The number of hunger strikers increased tenfold overnight, and casualties were reported. Malnourished, exposed to the glare of midday and the chill of spring evenings, fasting atop concrete with inadequate water supplies, protesters began to pass out after only thirty-six hours. The first ambulances drove onto Tiananmen Monday morning, necessitating the first cordons and security zones, the first closing of areas by student marshalls to the public.

By afternoon, the square was nearing capacity and its occupiers were exuberant. At three o'clock, the hour at which Gorbachev was to be greeted by President Yang Shangkun outside the Great Hall, a walking wall of demonstrators surged toward the building, until the army retreated inside the massive foyer. Not content, they charged the doors in waves. There was a collective whistle—of shock and delight—followed by a scramble. Some people, fearing the worst, withdrew, but most pushed forward for a better view. Eventually, the soldiers were ordered out to reassert control over a mob whose aggression had clearly caught officers unprepared. A standoff ensued, mediated by foreign TV crews and student leaders, who had to negotiate with their own legions to get them to back up to the sidewalk. The negotiations were surprisingly heated. Among the crowd were many Beijingers, often unemployed young men with tousled hair and dangling cigarettes, whose ideals were not those of the students, and who saw the assault on the Great Hall as an opportunity to express frustration and to raise hell. They had to be dissuaded from picking fights.

Incidents escalated, each more incendiary, more dangerous, than the one before. The square now held clinics for hunger strikers, rows of buses commandeered as shelters, makeshift tents and lean-tos to defend against the sun, lanes sealed by human chains to ensure the flow of ambulances, school flags unfurled on recently stripped poles. Parades of new recruits, predominantly from government and media work units but also representing universities in Tianjin, Shenyang and Shanghai, entered Tiananmen following prescribed routes, circled the rim once or twice, then set up camp to listen to speeches delivered from the stone base of the monument, now the movement's headquarters. Foreign camera crews filmed madly. Local camera crews filmed madly. (Each evening we raced back to campus to watch, in both Chinese and English, newscasts reporting actual news, including interviews with demonstrators.) Ordinary Beijingers wandered around the square smiling and staring and snapping pictures. How many ordinary Beijingers? A half million, then a million, then perhaps two million if the streets surrounding Tiananmen were included. There were people in baseball caps and sunglasses, beach hats and Hawaiian shirts, Mao suits and black slippers; families with children, grandmothers clutching water bottles, patriarchs reclining in pedicabs, school kids in red-and-white uniforms, out-of-towners who had planned to visit the Forbidden City and Mao's mausoleum (both were closed) but had to settle for witnessing an insurrection, in addition to an endless supply of young men whose idleness translated into excess energy and a minimal concern for personal well-being.

Not a policeman, not a soldier, not a single uniformed authority figure monitored this multitude or in any way attempted to control the marching, debating and celebrating that had turned Chang'an Avenue into a carnival and the gates of Zhongnanhai, where groups obligingly halted like lovers before a wishing well to cast invective upon Li Peng and Deng Xiaoping, into a jamboree. The throngs along Chang'an were so thick that pedestrian traffic stopped for half-hour stretches because of bicycle jams, stranded cars, stalled buses, trucks overflowing with incoming workers. Vendors of ice cream and soda camped stubbornly on the sidewalk, charging double, selling out in minutes, paying boys to squirm between bodies to fetch additional crates, which were then lugged back through the quagmire, creating more delays, more confusion, until finally people gave up and climbed trees, lampposts, the outer walls of the Forbidden City to glimpse from afar what they might never witness up close. It was hot and sticky. Strangers vied for the same piece of pavement, the same patch of grass, and by Thursday, especially in the streets farther away from the image-conscious eyes of student leaders, trucks and buses exploding with factory laborers raced at high speeds in no particular direction through bicycle lanes.

Torrential rain on Thursday afternoon slicked roads but did little to dampen the excitement. Still, Beijing was riding a high, and spirits remained buoyant. Reports of vandalism during the week were negligable. Many notorious *liu-mang* suspended petty crime activities to work as messengers, escorts and, of all things, neighborhood watches, while local grandmothers were off parading. Twice we watched, open-mouthed in astonishment, as altercations between bicyclists, normally the nastiest of spats, were resolved with smiles and mutual apologies.

Our college scrambled to keep pace. Dozens of students and a few teachers vanished onto Tiananmen early on. I went to Zhou Shuren's room several times, leaving notes. Mary's friend Zhang Naiying called from a hotel on Wednesday night to tell us that she was fine, and had just acted as a translator for leader Wang Dan and an American television network. Naiying had family near the square, meaning she had a place to sleep in the city and wouldn't be back on campus for a while. She thought what was happening was unbelievable but hesitated to be more specific over the phone. Several undergraduates dropped by to express similar views, or just to practice slogans in English: "Li Peng must step down!" and "Patriotism is not a crime!" Shu Sheyu visited late one night to drink bourbon.

"Is China changing?" I asked.

"I don't know about China," Shu answered, "but I think *I* am changing."

"For the better?"

He hesitated. "It depends," he replied with a shrug. "Ask me again in two weeks."

Shu proceeded to repeat the latest rumors that crossed Beijing faster than a phone call. Their source was often "Voice of America" reports or Western magazines; a recent issue of *Newsweek* had described a secret speech by Deng Xiaoping, in which he anticipated the slaughter of students to ensure national stability. The news was enough to make fists clench and mouths go dry: Zhao Ziyang was under arrest; Zhao had fled to Taiwan. Deng Xiaoping was dead; Deng had scurried from Beijing. Li Peng was washed up; Li had gathered support to form a new government. Soldiers were ready to move on the square; soldiers were refusing orders. Commanders were mutinying; commanders were rallying behind the Party. Each wild, wilder, wildest tidbit reverberated in our heads, making sleep fitful.

Our school marched on Wednesday and Thursday. Buses were provided by a suddenly supportive administration to transport protesters into the city where our banner was hoisted, arms were linked, and a squad of two hundred paraded along Chang'an Avenue under the stewardship of the charismatic Dean Shen, erstwhile opponent of all civil activism. Possibly the victim of a long memory, Shen Yanbing had initially commanded the English department to call off its boycott of classes and had personally rousted truants from their rooms, prophesying doom and warning against knocking on a door that one day might open. Now the dean devoted Wednesday morning to rooting out the reticent to ensure the buses would be packed. Dean Shen also wrote and signed a petition calling on the government not to discuss the students' demands but simply to accede to them outright. His about-face appeared to surprise only us. Shen Yanbing came over to Mary and me as we stood watching the vehicles load up.

"No classes today," he announced. "Even those taught by foreigners."

"Thanks," I said.

"Incredible things are happening," the dean continued, his mouth twitching. "Like nothing before. The government must listen to us now. The government must change!"

"Yes," we agreed.

"But foreign friends should not go near Tiananmen Square," he added. "It will be dangerous. We all may die. No one minds. I have to go. Sorry."

We wished him luck. Suddenly Dean Shen stopped, turned to Mary.

"You must get your new chapter in soon," he said, referring to a department book project. "Next week, okay?"

"Fine," Mary said to his back.

Later in the afternoon we waved to our colleagues from outside the Beijing Hotel and snapped photos of the vanguard: the heads of most departments, administration staff, with rows of teachers and students filling in the ranks. Dean Shen was uncomfortable before my camera—all the marchers were photographed by undercover police, usually well-dressed young men sporting plastic smiles and Japanese equipment—and the photos captured a melee of emotions on his face, an ambivalence at odds with his tardy but resolute plunge into the politics of the day.

Only Li Feigan held out. With school officially suspended on Thursday, Li had no grounds on which to demand a class, and was miffed.

"The students are being irresponsible," he complained.

"They are just making a parade," I answered.

"Occupying Tiananmen Square only angers the government," Li said, ignoring my gibe. "And forcing the cancellation of Gorbachev's plans embarrasses all of China, all of us. These tactics are counterproductive."

"The students see Gorbachev as an ally," I argued, "an example of reform and open-mindedness within a socialist system. The parallel is too easy."

"China is not the Soviet Union," Li said. "One cannot compare."

"China is China, right?"

He nodded. "The students cannot treat the leaders so disrespect-fully. Perhaps the leaders do not merit our respect, but we must give it to them anyway. The circumstances require compromise. Nothing will be changed this way. Nothing good will result." But the next morning Li and his wife, Dai Houxing, devoted the three hours of tenacious bus-riding, walking and shoving required to penetrate the rebel encampment.

"To have a look," Li admitted later, "out of curiosity, not agree-ment."

"Out of respect, maybe?" I suggested.

"Respect for whom?" he answered sharply.

That night Prime Minister Li Peng appeared on television with other members of the politbureau. Zhao Ziyang's absence from the proscenium—China's leading statesman had cast his lot in with the students and wept openly on camera during a bizarre visit to the square early Friday morning—declared the hard-liners the victors in the Party's internal battle. Li Peng announced that he was ordering troops into the capital.

When a brave man is angry, he draws his sword on someone stronger, while an angry coward draws his sword on someone weaker.

Once martial law had been declared on Saturday morning, regula-tions were flashed across TV screens, including warnings to foreigners not to attend demonstrations, take photographs or even talk with protesters. Locals were strongly advised to keep indoors. By noon, helicopters were swarming over Tiananmen Square, and reports were rife of troop columns rumbling along country roads toward the city. Nevertheless, locals opted decisively for the out-of-doors; huge crowds gathered on Chang'an Avenue to take offense at Li's ultimatum (a popular poster depicted the prime minister as a Nazi), heap scorn on the contention that Beijing was in the throes of anarchy and dis-miss, with a mix of incredulity and disappointment, the idea that the People's Liberation Army would ever act against the people. Once again, public opinion had galvanized swiftly into a body politic—in this case a civil-defense network—that dared and double-dared the enraged ruling cliques and advancing armies. If there was a flinch before Li's threats, it wasn't apparent, or perhaps was overwhelmed by a more strident emotion: disdain for a cowardly government and civic pride in defending one's home against aggressors.

Returning from town after lunch, our bus was ensnared in a traffic jam a mile from campus. Disembarking, we strolled up to a civilian roadblock outside the commerce institute. A seventy-vehicle column, each canvas-draped truck concealing twenty soldiers, had been halted and neutralized (air let out of the tires, radiator caps removed) by a mob that now engulfed the invaders. Though students were prominent in rank, they were few in number; statistically most relevant were the thousands of locals who had simply materialized on the scene. The mood was again carnivalesque: gangs of rumpled young men, couples steering baby carriages, old ladies proffering advice to the soldiers, toothless octogenarians wandering from truck to truck with hands clasped behind backs, somber teachers from nearby colleges whose glasses kept slipping down their noses, foreigners snapping photos and the standard allotment of kids who zigzagged between vehicles in mock battle, tree-branch swords in hand. Counter-propaganda was made at the open back of each truck; intellectuals, often undergraduates at our school, lectured the sweating recruits on the immorality of turning an army on its own population, while extemporaneous remarks from the crowd added a more informal rhetoric: "Your parents would be ashamed of you!" scolded locals. "Think about what you are doing!"

We spotted one of Mary's students, Bei Hua, sharing a joke with a uniformed driver, a fortyish man who, Hua informed us, had headed a detachment sent to our college the previous September to supervise a week of military training. The man had quaffed a few beers in the cafeteria one evening, thrilling a round table of blushing boys with dirty jokes and army lore. Remarkably, the soldiers, almost believing that they were being sent into Beijing to serve as movie extras, *were* ashamed and *did* agree that the People's Liberation Army, the PLA, was not an internal policing mechanism, not a weapon in intra-Party skirmishes. Even the officers, perched on cab sidesteps, offered no argument or resistence.

Though the standoff continued for several more hours, the result was a foregone conclusion: before cheering crowds, the column turned around one truck at a time and, forced to inch back up the highway around a junkyard of abandoned vehicles (including several of their own), retreated, a humiliated but relieved aggressor force. As they drove off, many soldiers offered the peace symbol, their AK-47s glinting in the late-afternoon light.

Then at midnight, a new column advanced on the city: tanks. An eyeball moon staved off the darkness, providing extra visibility for the crews constructing a barricade outside the north gate. Students dragged bleachers from the basketball courts to block the road, a laborious process made difficult because of a wide ditch crossed only by a rickety footbridge. The bleachers had to be hauled a quarter-kilometer to where the ditch closed, then pulled over the pavement to a position outside the gate. Aware that a tank could brush aside a wall of steel benches, students had also commandeered several trucks for reinforcement. But the trucks were parked *behind* the barricade; on the front line were a hundred bodies perched atop the bleachers, a pensive audience peering east into a narrowing corridor of street lamps.

All vehicles were stopped and searched; soldiers in civilian clothes had been discovered trying to pass through at other checkpoints. Fleets of motorcycles, operated by Beijing hooligans, buzzed up and down the road delivering messages and spying on the enemy. Observers kept to the school side of the ditch. We also probed the darkness for outlines and sounded the silence for warnings. Dean Shen flitted among us, entreating students back inside the gate where they would be protected; the army wouldn't dare trespass on a campus, even under martial law. He paused to inform Mary and me that "China is going to the dogs." The dean circled back a few minutes later to expand on the thought. "The government is crazy," he said. "Deng is senile. Li is a madman. All of them—crazy! They will kill us without a blink." Then, turning to the adoring students who had gathered to hang on his words, "Back inside! Back inside! You cannot fight tanks!"

Shu Sheyu interrupted his flirtation with some undergraduates to swagger over, his studied nonchalance betrayed by a worsening of his limp.

"What do you think, Shu?" I asked.

"I think it is bad," he replied. "Maybe we have gone too far." Then, grinning mischievously, he added, "Or not far enough. Who knows?"

We certainly didn't. Not that night and not the next afternoon, even after students staggered home from a clash in a distant suburb with a frightening tale: a crack police squad had lashed out at them with electric cattle prods, wounding sixty. Not even on Sunday evening could we say for sure when, at the barricade, eyes bleary from lack of sleep but legs twitching with adrenaline, punch-drunk from relentless flurries of rumors and forecasts of gloom, we fixed our gazes on the road following reports that a tank column had smashed an outer defense and was thundering toward the capital, toward us. It would soon be audible: first a rumble, then a roar and finally an earthquake, the noise obliterating everything. Frozen by dread, we would be incapable of either halting the mechanized assassins or getting out of harm's way. We just didn't know.

A country of weaklings, even if they have guns, can only massacre unarmed people; if the enemy is also armed, the issue is uncertain. Only then is true strength and weakness revealed.

"Standing up to a charge" used to strike me as empty talk, but now its truth has been proved, and it applies not only to grown-ups, but even to children. The time has gone when the "slaughter of innocents" was a crime. I suppose it will not be long before we toss infants into the air and catch them on the tips of our spears for fun.

Two more weeks passed before the tanks actually succeeded in penetrating Beijing. Classes sort of resumed, sort of didn't; the semester was basically ruined, but few would admit it. A third of the undergraduate class had already fled the campus. Others milled aimlessly about the dormitories like travelers stranded in an airport, while a tiny group, largely forgotten by the shell-shocked community, were still officially "disappeared." We visited the disappeared on Tiananmen Square, first outside their lean-to near the obelisk, then on the bus reserved for demonstrators from our institute. The square was a disaster, hectares of concrete littered with debris, mounds of rotting garbage, piles of clothes: the detritus of an abandoned shantytown. The tight security that had existed among the protestors before Li Peng ordered in the troops had dissolved; a student marshall approached us, accepted on face value our identities and requested that we autograph his jacket—a popular souvenir.

Unbeknownst to us, two of the movement's three principal leaders, Wang Dan and Wu'er Kaixi, had withdrawn from Tiananmen, taking with them the majority of the Beijing contingents. What was left, besides followers of the more militant Chai Ling, were kids from the provinces who had only just arrived in the capital, with nowhere else to sleep. These students were less politically astute, less likely to entertain arguments about the tactical advantages of ending the vigil. The northwest corner of the square was also now home to groups of workers whose late start in the movement, and specific grievances—their alliance with the students was based more on a common enemy than mutual concerns—left them with reservoirs of anger and determination. By the end of May, Tiananmen Square was occupied by a ragtag band of outlaws who continued to hold war councils and make petrol bombs and plot their own martyrdom with great courage but waning stamina and a blurred agenda. It was almost laughable that such a force, or more likely the symbolic import of it, as interpreted by city residents, should be keeping at bay the 300,000 PLA soldiers who had been pouring in from neighboring provinces and now ringed Beijing.

The half-dozen remaining undergraduates from our school certainly looked bedraggled. Mary knew one sophomore from a class she taught in the economics department. He was a nineteen-year-old from Hangzhou.

"How long have you been here?" she asked him.

"Eight days," he replied.

"Without a break?"

"I will not return to campus until Li Peng steps down," the boy said.

"How much longer—?" Mary began.

"Many students have left the square," he confessed. "They think the movement is finished. They think there is no hope. But we must stay until we have victory!"

"Maybe you've won already," I said.

The student smiled wanly. "Are there classes at the college?"

"A lot of students have fled the city," I admitted.

"I miss my family and friends," he continued. "And studying, and reading books. I have not spoken English in a month."

"Do you want us to bring you some books?" Mary asked.

"No use," the boy sighed. "I am too tired to read."

Before leaving, we offered a wad of money, collected from foreign teachers, and best wishes. The students escorted us back to the cordon. We signed their jackets as well.

The evening of Friday, June 2, was sultry, the sky smudged from pollution and the air tangy with exhaust fumes. Mary and I had just attended the professional debut of a young cellist at the Beijing Concert Hall—the first recital after six weeks of cancellations and closures—and were walking along Chang'an Avenue toward Tiananmen. Martial law notwithstanding, it was a lovely night to stroll. The sidewalk was a courtyard for the families who lived in the narrow alleys off the street. Men in undershirts smoked cigarettes while women watched over the fleets of bamboo prams nestled in the shade of trees. Traffic flowed, restaurants served meals, vendors hawked ice cream, and students played guitars, cooked pots of rice and dozed atop mattresses as part of their lazy picketing of Zhongnanhai, all without the presence of a vestige of civil authority.

We passed the north face of the Great Hall and crossed the street to the square. The "Goddess of Democracy," now in the third day of her reign, had been lit from below and seemed to shimmer in the twilight. The statue was rough-hewn but magnificent, a plaster and polystyrene figure of an athlete gripping a torch in plain view of the portrait of Mao Zedong that hung from the Gate of Heavenly Peace. The furor over the statue had not subsided since Wednesday. Government reaction was apoplectic ("China is not America!" the radio thundered), and Li Feigan, also assuming that the piece was modeled on the Statue of Liberty, declared it an "insult to the Chinese people." With the buses now gone, reclaimed by their drivers for use on the barricades that plugged major city arteries, rows of tents from Hong Kong served as shelter. By design, the tents stopped well before the Goddess, and the statue stood in stark isolation at the head of Tiananmen. Students had also tidied and swept the massive surface in anticipation of a fresh wave of the curious. The "Goddess of Democracy" was indeed engulfed by well-wishers: couples holding hands, fathers with children on their shoulders, families posed for photos. Again, there were rumors of battalions scurrying in the catacombs beneath Tiananmen and behind the walls of the Forbidden City, of battle-hardened troops preparing a tank assault, of Deng Xiaoping advocating high casualty figures to teach a lesson—but for some inexplicable reason, little of this mattered. The night was soft, the crowds were friendly, and it was impossible not to feel part of something grand, mysterious, evanescent.

Next morning, we learned that a squadron of unarmed soldiers had marched down Chang'an Avenue a few hours after our walk, only to be repelled, and ridiculed, by the same locals who had peacefully slurped ice creams and chewed seeds earlier in the evening. Tensions mounted during the day—the fourteenth of the siege—so that in late afternoon, with the heat intense and cicadas screeching, a number of us sought the relief of sports. On the way to the field I met Guo Yidong. Guo had been haunting the track since late April, his solitary figure—hands clasped, head bowed in contemplation—beyond the clamor of the moment.

"Well, Guo," I said as greeting, "you're managing all right?"

Guo hiccuped. "Perhaps not," he said. "I am feeling out of sorts. Odd. Even, let me see, misshapen."

"Misshapen?" I said.

"Outside of myself," he clarified, "like I have been removed from my skin and now, ahem, observe my body in a detached manner."

"Maybe it's the weather," I offered.

"Maybe," he agreed, arching an eyebrow. "More likely it is a concrete concern, something so animal it has the power to, let me see, disturb, no, perhaps even *obliterate* the intellect."

"Does it worry you?" I asked.

"I think it does," he admitted.

Our conversation was interrupted. "Soldiers are beating the students!" a woman shouted in Chinese. "Come to the south gate, everyone—soldiers are beating the students!" Beyond the gate, where the campus road intersected the highway into Beijing, students were working to waylay an army convoy. Trucks racing through the intersection had to swerve to dodge the rocks and bricks being launched at windshields and open windows. Projectiles also vanished into the slits between back flaps, causing them to rustle and divulge their occupants: lines of helmets, rows of rifle barrels. One student sniper, fed ammunition by cohorts who had dismantled an unmortared wall, was a dead-eye. He lobbed brick after brick high into the sky, a rainbow of apparently harmless objects that smashed the windshield of every third vehicle. Finally a truck, its driver blinded by splintering glass, swung off the road, veered into a scattering crowd, swiped a tree and jerked to a halt. That stalled the convoy, and it was instantly swarmed.

My fear that the soldiers would spring from their nests was far from hysterical; up ahead, near the commerce institute, rifle butts and leather belts were being used on protesters. Soon, however, the sheer number of locals, and their mood—the air crackled with violence—quelled any thought of heroic behavior on the part of the recruits. They stayed calm, and also silent, even those men who were bleeding from brick wounds. Officers addressed the rabble. "Beijing is in chaos," they explained. "Thugs and ruffians are looting shops, raping women, murdering babies. It is a counterrevolution. It is an attempt to undermine socialism, to allow foreigners to humiliate China." The army had their orders. The army would carry them out.

These soldiers, who stared at the foreigners in the crowd as if we wore hideous masks, spoke with thick accents, and I had to ask the student Bei Hua, prominent among the brick throwers, for a translation.

"This army is not local," he explained breathlessly. "They are from Manchuria."

"So?"

Bei Hua made a frantic gesture with both arms, as if to shoo away a cloud of bees. Then, wordless, he turned and sprinted back to his dormitory to borrow a bicycle.

Within an hour, Mary and I had lent our bikes to friends and watched as they pedaled past the stalled convoy toward the city. In our apartment we stared at the warnings being flashed across the television screen (Beijingers should stay indoors: anyone on the streets risked injury. The army would take whatever means necessary to regain control.) We dialed a few phone numbers, knocked on a few doors, and then, feeling completely useless, plunked ourselves down before a short-wave radio to absorb live BBC reports, bounced from Beijing to Hong Kong to Beijing, of a nightmare unfolding barely ten kilometers from where we sat.

The tanks roared past the institute at 2:00 A.M. The concrete floor of our living room trembled, and for the twenty minutes required to chew up the south highway it was impossible to speak or think or even see much through the dust clouds that darkened the street lamps. So feral, and so mounting was the noise that I was certain the brigade had turned onto the campus, headed for the dormitories. Students who crouched behind a wall counted sixty tanks moving at full clip in the direction of Tiananmen Square. Once the trembling had subsided, an Australian teacher, adept at probing short-wave static for signals, acted as information officer, and the remaining hours of the night were spent in dire wakefulness.

At eight o'clock Sunday morning, the television greeted Beijingers with footage of armored vehicles toppling the "Goddess of Democracy." Shortly afterward, we joined a crowd outside the men's dormitory to listen to "Voice of America" reports from an open window. A character poster hung from a neighboring room: "June 4, 1989—the day China died." People wept, heads lowered, arms limp at sides. Dazed, reeling from the scale of the carnage, few expressed outrage or fury or even the desire, welling in me like lust, to bloody a face, crack a rib, watch Deng Xiaoping and Li Peng writhe in agony as bereaved loved ones took their revenge.

Shu Sheyu wandered over to us, his eyes swollen. "'I love China,'" he quoted, "'but who loves me?'" Then, noting our puzzlement, "Lu Xun, after another massacre of students." He moved on to a group of friends. Though dreading the four walls of our apartment, we felt uncomfortable witnessing such grief, and decided to leave. Zhao Zhenkai, the former London embassy staffer, squatted under a tree. I approached to ask if he was all right—Zhao had borrowed my bike the previous night—but stopped short before his anguished face. He spoke in Chinese, and then, focusing my image through fogged lenses, in English. "The soldiers killed everybody," he said. "On Chang'an, in the side streets. I watched them fire into crowds. A woman with a baby fell beside me.... I tried to help her up ..." I nodded, but Zhao took no notice. "I didn't think they would do this," he continued. "I didn't think they would kill so many people...." Neither of us moved or spoke. Mercifully, a man appeared at the window and launched into a synopsis of the clearing of Tiananmen, his words falling on cautious silence, in stark contrast to the hurrahs and shouts that had enlivened previous rallies. But then this was not a rally; it was a wake.

Sunday afternoon witnessed the flight of hundreds of students from campus, some downtown to catch a train (risky, given the reports of troops sniping at civilians outside the station) and others, posses- sions slung over their shoulders, moving in the opposite direction, on foot, toward a city more than one hundred kilometers away. A few undergraduates knocked on our door to say goodbye, but most, wary of venturing near the foreigners' dormitory, simply vanished.

Another army column tore up the south highway that night and was challenged outside the commerce institute, where a barricade of articulated buses slowed the armored personnel carriers long enough to permit an attack. We listened to the gunfire from our balcony, watched the lower margin of the sky brighten when a shell scorched shops near the gate. Two students were killed, and next morning fires blazed inside the mangled buses, now ripped in half, and an army jeep already stripped of its engine. A wreath lay where a body had fallen; the grass was bloody, still compressed from the efforts of friends to drag the corpse to the guardhouse.

It rained on Monday and Tuesday, and we restricted ourselves to the neighborhood around the college, not imprisoned—many West- erners stole about the city on bicycle—but severely addled. Conversa- tion was all gossip, which we wearily ingested, dutifully exaggerated, then passed on: troops had orders to search Beijing campuses; a civil war between divisions who had perpetrated the massacre and those who had opposed it was imminent; warlordism and the fragmentation of the country was inevitable; Li Peng had been shot in the leg; Deng was dead (again); the American embassy was going to be stormed to recapture Fang Lizhi and his wife, Li Shuxian; Wu'er Kaixi had been executed; Chai Ling was in jail; the army was gunning for foreigners near the main embassy compound....

Zhou Shuren visited us at eleven o'clock Monday night. He wore a Mao suit and his hair was cropped, like a country bumpkin. Refusing a beer, Zhou paced the room.

"I must leave Beijing tonight," he said. "The police are looking for me."

"Why, Zhou?" Mary asked.

His answer was a whisper. "I have stayed with friends the last two weeks, at an art institute across the city. Many of these friends worked on the 'Goddess of Democracy.' Our pictures were taken by secret police."

"Were you on the square Saturday night?" I asked.

"That's right," he replied. "On the square when the army began to shoot people. I tried to fight back but got trapped in an alleyway by a tank. For two hours the tank didn't move. I didn't move either. Then it was dawn. All morning I helped carry bleeding bodies to the hospitals ..." Zhou sobbed, stared down at his hands. Mary and I found an excuse to slip into the kitchen for a moment.

"Where will you go?" I eventually asked.

"Tibet," he answered, brushing imaginary hair from his face. "Canada. Iceland. It doesn't matter."

We both muttered condolences.

"China is shit," Zhou said. "Only crazy people live here, or stupid people like me." Before leaving he pulled out three music cassettes that he had borrowed months before. "Sorry I kept the tapes so long."

Zhang Naiying also vanished. Colleagues claimed the student Bei Hua had been arrested. Another foreign teacher, friends with the tired young undergraduate from Hangzhou we had chatted with on Tiananmen, reported that several people had seen the boy carried off on a stretcher. Shu Sheyu, always keen to trade in rumors, languished in our apartment for three straight evenings, drinking, poking at the foods that kept arriving from the refrigerators of evacuated foreigners, dialing phone numbers—his younger brother, on the square as of midnight June 3, had yet to reappear—and watching propaganda on television. Reality had been under sustained assault since the first images of the smashed Goddess Sunday morning: no one had died on Tiananmen Square; no one had died along Chang'an Avenue; only two hundred people were killed, most of them brave soldiers; a gang of thugs had committed heinous crimes; the counterrevolution had conspired to destroy the country and negate the Party; all Beijingers welcomed the restoration of order. The propaganda was absurdly transparent—footage of the violence, featuring a digital reading of the time in the corner, would be shown with an overdub claiming a different hour, often day instead of night, for when the event was supposed to have occurred. Shu studied it, though, partly to glean information from slipsups in the official version and partly out of habit. Perhaps it was the language barrier that prevented us from staring at the screen; perhaps it was the knowledge, gained in calls from foreigners who had fled campus for a hotel hooked up to CNN television, that we would soon be privy to other images, less doctored, less infuriating. Twice I was about to ask Shu Sheyu whether now, two weeks later, he knew if he had changed for better or for worse, but both times the look on his highly expressive face was too stark.

Wednesday afternoon, having just agreed to be evacuated to Hong Kong the next morning, I walked from our barren campus over to the desolate commerce institute to take photos of the gutted vehicles and charred buses. I also paused before the wreath to the dead student, which was now festooned with flowers and poetic eulogies. The poems were written in red and black ink, using a personalized script that, unlike generic ideographs, could have been traced to an individual. On the fence beside the wreath was a pair of glasses, flecked with blood, one lens shattered. I stared at the eyes, the outline of the body in the grass, until the gazes of locals hastened my departure.

Dean Shen tried avoiding me when I approached him on the pathway to say goodbye. Rumor had it that Shen Yanbing had suffered a nervous breakdown on Sunday and been hospitalized. But I wondered; the dean looked no more manic than usual.

"The students went too far!" he shouted, waving his arms. "They made the old men furious. Now we are all finished!"

"All of you?" I said.

"I may be arrested at any moment," Dean Shen continued. "I wrote a petition, made other teachers sign it. I led the march onto Tiananmen Square. They will come for me first. The students went too far!"

"I'm sorry," I said.

"Back in April I told them this. Back in April. Why didn't someone stop us?" The dean paused. "What about Mary's chapters for the intensive reading book?" he asked. "I could send my assistant to pick the work up. I could—"

I told Dean Shen that Mary would mail the remaining pages and shook his hand. He mumbled about the postal system not being reliable; censors opened parcels from abroad and destroyed important documents.

Li Feigan saw us off the next morning. "China will change," he offered in a voice betrayed by the pallor of his face. "But very slowly. Several generations must wait until the people are better educated regarding human rights and alternative political systems." Mary and I nodded weakly; it was 5:45 A.M., and we hadn't slept in days. At the south gate, the bus jerked to a halt, then withdrew behind a wall to let another military convoy past the college, truck tires churning up fountains of spray. In three hours, fêted on croissants and coffee, wished a pleasant voyage and a quick return to the Middle Kingdom, we would be in Hong Kong, where we would hole up in a matchbox hotel room for a week to watch the massacre on television, watch it ruthlessly, obsessively, until our eyes squeezed shut to ward off the dreadful, familiar, mundane images.

I am always more distressed and worried by the death of a friend or student if I do not know when, where, and how he died. And I imagine that from their point of view to perish at the hands of a few butchers in a dark room is more bitter than dying in public.

PART III

PENANCE

1

BEI HUA

Bei Hua caused trouble on April 5, 1990, the Qingming Festival of hommage to deceased ancestors, by attempting to place a flower on Tiananmen Square. The square was closed to the public in the afternoon for a ceremony performed by middle-school children. Mary and I loitered among the undercover cops, foreign journalists, grieving parents, bitter students and idle curious who stood at the periphery. Meanwhile, Bei Hua descended into the passageway below Chang'an Avenue, approached the wall of soldiers and asked politely to be allowed through in order to lay a white carnation on the balustrade of the Monument to the People's Heroes. Why did he want to do that? a soldier asked. Because it is Qingming, Hua replied. Our duty is to show respect for the souls of the dead. For this impertinence, Bei Hua was handcuffed, bundled into a van and driven to a nearby police station.

Hua told me the story himself later that evening. I was headed to the sports ground for a walk. Half the college had suddenly materialized outdoors. With the day nearly over, people felt they could venture into the night air without fear of political repercussions. The relief should have released stores of cheer, but instead, the badminton games along the paths were joyless and most strollers exercised in isolation, avoiding gatherings. I was about to merge with traffic on the track when Bei Hua called from the shadow of a bleacher. Without waiting, he stole around a corner into an empty alley. Hua then launched into a breathless account of the arrest, an explosion of words punctuated by wild-eyed glances over my shoulder to see if anyone was observing us. The president of the institute, he explained, had been summoned to the station to collect him—a humiliation designed to ensure the administration's wrath would fall on the student. A squad of soldiers was now stationed outside the north gate, hassling anyone who left campus to so much as buy a yogurt in a local shop.

Hua had more news. "I cannot visit you and Mary any more," he said. "It is dangerous to be seen with foreigners."

"Hua?"

"The administration wants me to confess that you forced me to go down to Tiananmen Square today. They want to report back to the Public Security Bureau that it was an outside influence that caused my bad thoughts."

I nodded.

"They also know about Monday," Hua added in a whisper.

Earlier in the week, Mary and I had, as was our custom, invited a student to eat with us in the campus restaurant. This Monday our guest had been Bei Hua. Apart from the usual besotted revelers and mounds of animal bones on the floor, two things about the meal stood out in my memory. First, Bei Hua had ordered the one dish on the menu we found inedible, beef tendons in brown sauce that looked like plastic tubing in mud. As well, Hua had raised the subject of Qing-ming Festival and hinted that he would not be locking himself in his room for the day. We had listened to his plan of joining marchers from other universities—a march that never materialized—to protest the massacre, and then flatly, pointedly, told him not to go unless he was absolutely sure there would be thousands of others present. An isolated act of defiance would be senseless, we maintained. Hua had only nodded, smiled his affable smile and finished the last plastic tube.

"The dinner was evidence?" I guessed.

"We were seen," he explained.

"Eating beef tendons?"

"I am going to be expelled," Hua said, already moving away from me. "Maybe sent to prison. The administration hasn't decided yet. I must go."

"I'm sorry, Hua."

"They want me to say I am under your influence."

"Because of literature class?"

"W. B. Yeats is a great poet," he confirmed. Then, eyes welling, "Say goodbye to Mary. I will never see either of you again. I will be forced to leave Beijing and return to my hometown. I will never have a chance to speak English or talk to foreigners. I will never—"

"Go," I said.

"I blame no one."

"It's okay, Hua."

He turned to leave. "Thank you for the dinner on Monday," he said. "It was delicious."

Bei Hua was lucky to have lasted to his senior year. His iconoclasm was so habitual that the administration must have often been tempted to declare him irredeemable and send him packing. Hua had given them ample ammunition. A disc jockey at the college "radio station"—a network of loudspeakers, installed during the Cultural Revolution to pound the ideology-of-the-month into revolutionaries—Hua had ruffled feathers months before Tiananmen by spicing an all-music program with his random thoughts on life on a small Beijing campus. He was banned from the air during the early weeks of the movement for reading reports of student activities, reinstated by the flip-flopping administration early in the week of Gorbachev's visit and told again point-blank on the advent of martial law to shut up or else.

Biking into the city the night of the massacre, Hua did his best to be killed or arrested, staying on Tiananmen Square until shortly before dawn, when negotiators arranged with the army for the withdrawal of the remaining protesters. Next he roamed downtown for two days, never actually battling soldiers but refusing to retreat to the sanctuary of the campus. To further his reputation, Bei Hua began his final undergraduate year by accepting a month-long apprenticeship at a Beijing radio station, thereby conveniently missing the weeks of intensive "reeducation" endured by everyone at the institute at the beginning of the fall semester. Now it was April, and Hua appeared to be gearing up for the round of anniversaries. Why not just toss the boy out? The issue was hardly patronage. Bei Hua was not from Beijing, not the son of an important official, not the relative of a professor, not even on a scholarship (his work unit was paying the fees). He was, in short, a nobody, as easy to expel as reality was to alter.

The problem appeared to be personality. Hua was so disarmingly pleasant and likable that college authorities could neither hate the senior nor, more important, reduce him to an abstraction. Bei Hua was too obviously Bei Hua: everybody knew him, and knew what he was like. He was, first of all, the finest student in the graduating class. His English, learned as a teenager from "Voice of America" broadcasts, was frequently ungrammatical but always expressive, rich in diction and spiced with slang. Blessed with a good ear, Hua had mastered a flat American accent. Not only did he sound like a radio-show host, he looked like one; in order to force his mouth to flute bizarre English vowel combinations, the twenty-two-year-old had to puff up his chest and lower his chin, his brow knitting from the strain. Foreigners encountering him for the first time did a double-take, while fellow undergraduates were awed by such mimicry. But Hua's skills transcended imitation. He was a fine singer (specializing in early Beatles and John Denver), a decent guitar player, and he had won the college public-speaking contest four years in a row. His profile on campus was high, yet his enemies were few, despite the troubles his activism had caused.

What distinguished Bei Hua most, however, was his background. Born in Jilin province, he was abandoned as a baby by his Red Guard parents, who had vanished into the hinterlands to perpetuate Mao's revolution and never returned. Shuffled from aunt to aunt, the boy eventually wound up in an orphanage—rare in a country where the social net of the family was virtually omnipresent—in the capital city of Changchun, notable for its acrid pollution. At age fourteen, Hua was rediscovered by another relative and went to live with her at a high school work unit. When that relative also died, he was adopted, in effect, by the work unit itself, becoming the ward of a socialist paradigm. That paradigm was now sponsoring his education in Beijing, in return for a binding seven-year contract to teach English at the school upon completion of his degree. The repeated collapse of personal support systems might have devastated another young man, encouraging an even greater dependence on father figures and the archetypal fatherland. But in Hua's case, the opposite occurred. Freed from the net, he swam vigorously, happily, as a solo figure, an orphan in a culture obsessed with families.

Four nights after Qingming, Bei Hua called from the reception area in our dormitory to ask if he could visit. I questioned the wisdom of his signing in at the desk, suggesting instead that we meet on the track. Hua answered that he didn't mind registering, and that he was accompanied by a friend, Zheng Bo. I told them to come up.

Zheng Bo was also my student. As the powerful monitor of the leading senior class, during the student movement Bo had repeatedly done the department's bidding, denouncing the demonstrations, pressuring classmates to end the boycott, even, it was rumored, providing the names of students who had camped on Tiananmen and fought the army. He was bright and ambitious, well connected and looked most comfortable in a Mao suit. Yet Zheng Bo was also Bei Hua's protector. They were not only roommates but friends, and if any one individual had so far saved Bei Hua from expulsion, it was probably Bo. How this added up, if it did, was beyond my comprehension.

Side by side, Bei and Zheng looked like a youthful Abbott and Costello. Zheng Bo was short and lumpish, hobbled by poor posture and duck feet. His head was egg-shaped, hair closely cropped, and while his features were not pudgy (no undergraduate ate well enough to get fat), they were naturally soft, ripe to blossom into the jowly cheeks and double chin of a contented mandarin. Bo wore his only jacket, two sizes too small, and a brown shirt buttoned to the collar. Bei Hua was, in contrast, six feet tall, loose and gangly like a Toronto teenager, with a high forehead, wavy hair and bad skin. Unlike Zheng

Bo, who donned glasses in class but preferred to squint in private, Hua was never seen, and probably could not himself see, without his black-rimmed spectacles, which he had to push back into position every few minutes. Hua owned three shirts and two pairs of pants; tonight he was dressed in his white shirt, collar open, and the black pants that halted above his ankles, exposing translucent socks. I seated them on the couch, poured tea and insisted they try a chocolate Easter egg (fresh box). Hua, who had been in our apartment several times last year, scanned the living room.

"Nice room," he said.

"Yes."

"Very comfortable."

"We're fortunate to live here."

"Is it okay to talk?" he asked.

Zheng Bo sniggered.

"I think so," I said. "Nobody's sure."

"The administration hasn't decided yet if they will expel me," Hua began, unwrapping an egg. "They are delaying their decision."

"Is that good?"

"Maybe," he answered. "But I don't think I care. Because of my situation, it does not matter if I am told to leave. Even without a degree, I will still have to return to my work unit for seven years. Students who receive their job assignment from the department have more worries than me."

"Has the department assigned jobs?"

"Not yet," Zheng Bo replied quickly.

"Do you know what your job will be, Bo?" I asked on a hunch.

Zheng Bo described a dream position with a Beijing organization devoted to international trade, which included a large monthly salary and accommodation. He would be invited abroad by foreign companies that wished to do business inside the country and therefore had to go through the organization (and several more like it) to commence negotiations. His future promised banquets, gifts, favors, visits to distant lands.

"Nice job," I said.

He smiled graciously.

"Have other students found nice jobs?"

"April is still too early for the department to make assignments," Bo repeated.

"Zheng Bo has *guanxi*," Hua offered.

"And a Beijing residency card?" I said.

It was virtually impossible to live in the capital without a residency card. Foreign firms, until recently free to hire whomever they liked, were now forbidden even to interview prospective employees from outside the city. Government organizations were also restricted, with rare exceptions. Zheng Bo was, I knew, from Jiangxi province.

"The card is being arranged," he said, still smiling.

Bo must indeed have had connections, *guanxi*.

"Have another egg," I said.

More tea was poured, more chocolates were peeled. Bei Hua repositioned his glasses, complimented me again on the room, cleared his throat. Zheng Bo, his close friend, sat closely beside him, slurping tea. I put the kettle on to boil, then visited Mary in the bedroom where she was correcting essays.

"It was nice of you to drop by, Bo," I announced when I returned. "But you must be busy. Don't feel obliged to stay."

"Thank you," he said, not moving.

I glanced at Hua. "Should you really *be* here?" I said in exasperation. "Won't this provide further evidence that we influenced your Qingming protest?" Then, before he could answer, I turned to Zheng Bo. "Do *you* think we were behind Hua's white carnation?"

"Of course not," he answered firmly. "The administration has a wrong policy." Bo paused, having said too much already, but then continued. "Their approach to the problem is not very logical. We are told to attend classes given by foreign teachers, to copy their pronunciation and accents. This *is* being influenced," he added, clenching a fist in passion. "When is it good, when is it bad?"

I poured tea.

"Bei Hua is emotional," he said, speaking as if Hua were a prisoner at a parole hearing. "He lacks discipline and a sense of patriotism. But he has no bad feelings toward our country. And he acts in isolation. No one else is involved."

Hua, to my disbelief, was grinning from ear to ear. "I am a poor quality socialist," he confirmed. "Made in Taiwan, perhaps."

They both laughed at the joke, clearly popular among students. Encouraged silently by Zheng Bo, Bei Hua finally asked the question that had motivated the visit.

"Is it true that in Canada a person must only appear at a border and he will be accepted as a refugee?"

"Where did you hear this?"

"A magazine article that I read. It said some people had jumped from a boat and washed up on the shores of Canada, without passports or identification. These people were allowed to stay in the country."

"Do you mean the Sikhs in Nova Scotia?"

"Possibly."

"They almost drowned, Hua. It was a crazy thing to do."

"The article said the Canadian government would not turn them away. They would be political refugees."

"Maybe," I admitted.

"And these people had no passports?"

"Apparently not."

"Just made it to Canada," Hua said, his voice steely with determination, "or even to a Canadian embassy? Could a person perhaps declare himself a refugee at an embassy, and become Canadian?"

"These are hard questions to answer," I stammered. "Especially now, after what happened on Qingming ..."

"Friendly conversation," he said. "It is okay."

I looked to Zheng Bo. He blinked.

"It would have to be an embassy in a third country," I offered quietly. "Not here in Beijing, that's for sure. They couldn't help you—I mean, help the person."

"What about Fang Lizhi?" Bo asked, speaking of the astrophysicist who was still being sheltered in the American embassy.

"Fang is special."

"Of course," he nodded.

"It would have to be Japan or Taiwan or—"

"Hong Kong?" Hua said.

"Maybe. I don't know. I'm not an immigration lawyer."

Hua gulped his tea, then unwrapped and ate a fifth chocolate egg. "But it is certain that the refugee would not need a passport to be accepted?" he said.

I wanted to end the conversation. "In some countries," I said, "ordinary citizens are not allowed to have passports. The government uses the document as a weapon, to ensure compliant behavior. Canada would understand the predicament of a refugee who escaped from an oppressive government. Immigration officials would not refuse a claimant because he had no passport."

Hua sighed and sat back in the couch. Zheng Bo, his goitrous eyes fixed on the carpet, also stirred, asking if he could use our toilet.

"It's *very* dangerous, Hua," I whispered once we were alone. "People get killed trying those things."

Though Bei Hua nodded, he waited until his chaperon reappeared before speaking. "Could I ask your advice?" he said.

"Sure."

"What do you think a person should do if he would rather die than continue to live in his homeland?"

I started to sweat.

"I love my country," he continued. "I want to be buried in my hometown. But I also cannot live here any more. Either I escape, or I die. It is simple."

"No, it's not," I protested.

"Why am I not permitted to see the world?" Hua asked. "Why do teachers show us maps of other countries, teach us their histories, allow us to read books and watch movies about these places, but then the government never permits us to leave? Is curiosity unpatriotic?"

"A country is not a prison," Zheng Bo said.

I winced.

"So what should Hua do?"

"Why Hua, Bo?" I said sharply. "Why not yourself?"

"I don't mind it here." He shrugged. "I have family and connections. My future is secure. But Bei Hua is different. He is out of place. There is a word ..."

"Misfit," Hua chimed in.

"And you want to help him?" I said to Bo.

Now *I* was discussing Bei Hua like a parole officer. But Zheng Bo understood the question. "He is a friend," he replied simply. "In this society you help who you know, mostly family. Since Hua is an orphan, he is vulnerable."

"I am a misfit," Hua declared. "No room for me in the workers' paradise. I must leave, or else I will get killed, or locked in a prison with Wei Jingsheng and the other troublemakers."

Zheng Bo switched languages to tell his classmate quite ferociously to keep quiet.

Hua blanched. "Well," he said to me. "Do you have any excellent advice?"

"Apply to graduate schools in the States?" I said.

"A new regulation says that undergraduates must wait five years before making application to study abroad."

I knew that.

"Get a job with a joint-venture company that might send you to their country for training?"

"I have no residency card for Beijing."

I knew that.

"Find a joint-venture in Changchun?"

"There aren't many."

I knew that.

"Try switching jobs to a company that has overseas contacts? That way you might find a—"

"I must teach at my work unit for seven years."

I knew that.

"Buy yourself out of the contract?"

He was silent.

Now covered in a film of sweat, I pretended to ponder. Next I raised both hands to sculpt the air with my thoughts. Hua leaned forward in anticipation. His smile was confident, as if success were assured now that he had confessed his dilemma to a foreigner. Even Mary, hidden behind a concrete wall, rustled papers. Only Zheng Bo saw through me; he skinned the final chocolate egg, his expression vague.

"Be patient, Hua," I muttered.

Pain spread across my student's face like a shadow over a field. Removing his glasses, he tried to scrub the shadow off. I felt nauseated. But, ever gallant, Hua rose and shook my hand.

"Thank you for the tea," he said. "You and Mary are very kind."

I saw them to the door. "Is it really desperate?" I asked.

"Not desperate," Bo answered quickly.

"I think so," Hua corrected.

Mary emerged from the bedroom. Together we listened to the footsteps retreat down the stairwell. Neither of us dared to make eye contact. *Wei Jingsheng, Wei Jingsheng, Wei Jingsheng,* I intoned silently. What was in a name?

In February 1989, one of Mary's students had been arrested on Tiananmen Square after she was spotted chatting with American tourists late at night, probably to improve her English. The young woman was already wayward in her studies, busy with part-time jobs and boyfriends, and the administration hastily expelled her from the institute. Rather than emphasize the student's absenteeism or poor grades, however, a bulletin was posted linking her expulsion to the arrest and also to the girl's "frequent contact with foreigners." Within hours, a rumor was circulating the dormitories that the woman had contracted AIDS from a foreigner. Both the choice of illness and carrier were significant: AIDS was a disease of impurity, the literal and symbolic by-product of contact with contaminated, impure people. The student's fate presented a cautionary tale. Though the message regarding advisable levels of exposure to foreigners had always been loud (if not clear) at our college, it had gone unheeded during the nine months leading up to the June 4 massacre. But now, nine months *after* the crackdown, things appeared to be reverting to an earlier, darker state of hysteria. Consequently, some acquaintances decided that the dangers of fraternizing with Mary and me were too great. Those individuals who accepted the risk did so consciously, as a quiet gesture of courage and protest.

And what of Bei Hua: would he also suddenly contract a contagious disease and need to be expunged? The decision would probably be Dean Shen's. He held the power, as head of the department Bei Hua studied in and as a senior Party member. But the dean was himself in disgrace, still waiting to hear what punishment he would suffer for his Tiananmen activities. Shen Yanbing was even more frantic in April than he had been in February, when, handing us our schedules, he had specified, "Teach anything you like, but *don't* talk about the Turmoil. Anything else is okay. But no politics or East-West business or differences between cultures. And no Turmoil! Students want to improve their American accents and learn the newest words. They love America!" Then, as if offering a self-criticism at a Party struggle session, Dean Shen had added, "The students *think* they love America. We all think we do. We must be wrong. The Turmoil was crazy. Hurt the country's stability. Hurt me badly. I am finished. Maybe to jail, maybe loss of job. Finished!"

The dean had recently launched a crusade to see that undergraduates would have neither the time nor energy to brood over last year. The idea was to fill their waking hours with a grinding schedule of sports meets, song and speech contests, drama nights and movie marathons. We met Shen Yanbing at a play competition where he was one of the judges.

"Good activity," he told us privately. "Students must not be allowed to think about what happened. Mention *nothing* about the Turmoil in your classes, okay?"

"Okay," we said.

"Some people are in trouble," he explained. "Big trouble, like me. We must be careful. Foreigners also. Not to get mixed up in trouble. What a terrible place, eh?"

That night, Shen Yanbing awarded second prize to a skit written and performed by two undergraduates and a foreign student. The skit was a satire of certain national characteristics, and featured the foreigner bowing slavishly before a poster of model socialist Lei Feng while locals duped him of his money and possessions. Next day it was announced that the dean had chosen the play to represent our school at a Beijing-wide contest to be held in a week. The buzz around the department was deafening; everyone was stunned, including the students whose careers would be in jeopardy if the skit were criticized (which it surely would be). True to form, the afternoon before the contest Dean Shen rose before an assembly and withdrew the play, scolding its authors for their recklessness. Our institute would go unrepresented at the competition, a loss of face the department chief blamed on the teenagers who had created such a dangerous skit, a skit that he had been forced to enjoy, promote, agonize over, then cancel and denounce.

Bei Hua's fate was in this man's hands?

2

THE OLD HUNDRED NAMES

April was the month at the college when students and teachers alike focused their thoughts on the future. Job assignments, graduate schools, ESL and GRE exams,* scholarships abroad, transfers, apartment upgrades all suddenly loomed, and individuals had to react swiftly. Too hesitant a response and a classroom, dormitory, even a career would be assigned without consultation. Too hasty a move, on the other hand, was akin to bidding excessively in a card game; anxiety revealed underlying desperation, which marked a player as vulnerable. The collegian who aspired to take part in determining his or her future had to be a shark, gifted at the poker face and bluff. In April, ears were bent, *guanxi* was used, gifts appeared on tables, and everybody paid keen attention to what everybody else was doing while maintaining a stance of stiff indifference, studied nonchalance, lest one gave the impression that one's life was a matter of some importance, a decidedly bourgeois notion.

*Both the English as a Second Language (ESL) and the Graduate Record Examination (GRE) are required by most American universities willing to accept foreign students.

Events the previous spring had curbed some of the cynicism that fueled the usual bartering and bribing. Postmassacre paralysis had then compounded the problem. With universities under investigation and school officials flinching in anticipation of government blows, most deals and arrangements—like Guo Yidong's transfer to the college of traditional medicine—were canceled. Barely half the 1989 graduating class received job assignments, and seniors had to return to campus in September to sit the exams they had missed in June. Many remained in limbo for months, either languishing at home or else engaged in private, and often frowned upon, pastimes. The whole thing was a mess, and all parties vowed it would not be repeated in 1990.

The date was April 18. Hu Yaobang had been dead for 368 days, and the tentative first demonstrations on Tiananmen Square were already a year in the past. The weather twelve months ago had cooperated in luring people from their rooms. Tonight, though, a threatening sky seemed to counsel restraint. Li Feigan's brisk knock on our door was lost in the drumming of rain on the roof and memories in my head. When I finally opened the door, it was as a precaution.

"I knocked several times," Li complained, entering before either his wife, Dai Houxing, or Yu Wei. "We were worried that you and Mary had gone into the city."

"Why would we have done that?"

"Foreigners in Beijing will want to express their outrage by standing on Tiananmen Square when local people do not dare," he replied. "This will make them feel superior."

"Sorry I was slow to answer," I said.

He handed me his soaked jacket.

"Did you sign in downstairs?" I asked.

"No need," Li said. "I am well known on campus."

"Li is famous," Houxing confirmed.

"Terrible weather," Mary said.

"Normal for April," he explained.

"But last year—?"

"Last year was different."

"No one could understand the weather last spring," Yu Wei offered, wiping her glasses on her sleeve. "This spring is more natural for us."

"Natural?"

"What we are used to," she clarified.

"I nearly fell in a muddy ditch this afternoon," I said, ushering guests into the living room. "That same ditch outside the north gate. Why do they keep digging, refilling and digging it over again. What's the point?"

"Asian Games," Li said.

"Could you be more specific?"

He could not. All massive construction and repair jobs around Beijing were related to the Asian Games, now five months away. The government's campaign to ensure that the city would be utterly transformed by September was little more than an epic version of Dean Shen's talent nights. Attention was being diverted; heads were being stuffed with ardent thoughts of handball courts and soccer fields, apartments to house athletes, widened avenues to funnel tourists. Thousands of workers from Shandong and Anhui provinces were being brought to the capital to erect fake walls around unsightly housing divisions, tear up pavement, lay pavement, dig ditches, fill ditches in. The games would demonstrate Beijing's superiority as an urban center and rubber-stamp the country's modernization drive. If everyone "pulled together," the Asian Games might even prove that, recent setbacks in Eastern Europe notwithstanding, the future of socialism under the aegis of the Communist Party was bright. "Pulling together," in this instance, meant some free labor and a few absurd cosmetic alterations (closed-in balconies, a favorite way of creating extra space in an apartment, were banned along major roads). But mostly it meant money: lotteries for the games, benefits for the games, "voluntary" deductions from pay packets for the games, "donations" from each work unit for the games, "contributions" by international hotels and businesses for the games, delays in repairs to a primitive city infrastructure to divert the cash to the games. The appetite for hard currency was insatiable. Compromised by its own propaganda, the government had no choice but to keep squeezing the public, siphoning scarce funds from other budgets, ignoring the empty hotels and barren tourist sites in order to build new hotels and new tourist attractions.

"The games are important to the leadership," Li said without enthusiasm. "To prove that they are capable of managing an international event."

"Manage sports," Houxing said mischievously, "but not pigeons."

We asked.

"Officials have trained pigeons for the Asian Games," Houxing began, ignoring her husband's frown. "The birds practice in a village outside Beijing. But local people keep shooting the birds."

"What sports do the pigeons play?" I said.

"Not sports!" she laughed. "For a special purpose. The pigeons fly around and around and come home."

"Locals are shooting homing pigeons?"

She nodded. "Officials get very angry. 'Don't shoot Asian Games pigeons!' they tell the peasants."

"What do the peasants say?"

"They cannot tell the difference between Asian Games pigeons and ordinary pigeons."

"Is there a difference?" Mary inquired.

"The government marks Asian Games pigeons on their wings," Li said. "The paint is clear and unambiguous. Still, locals claim they only notice the marking after it is too late."

"Too late?"

"Pigeons are delicious," Yu Wei said.

"But expensive to train," Li added. "Much money is spent teaching the pigeons to perform the trick. Officials want to use the birds in the opening ceremony. But locals do not care. They like the taste of pigeon meat."

"Serious problem," I said.

"The government has threatened to arrest any peasants who shoot Asian Games pigeons."

"What will be the charge—counterrevolutionary eating habits?"

Li smiled tightly. Mary poured drinks while I whisked out the starters: salami, Swiss cheese, bread.

"Western food," I said. "As promised."

"Very delicious," Houxing predicted, pushing hair back from her face. Her chattiness tonight was unusual, and Mary and I were both pleased. Li, in contrast, seemed subdued. He looked haggard, weighed down by troubles. For a man who prided himself on never showing his hand, this signified either a new level of ease around us, where he felt no need to mask his emotional state, or a new level of unease, which he could no longer suppress.

"These are only to start," I explained. "The main course is more substantial."

"Also Western?" Li asked, sniffing a piece of salami.

"A little nostalgia," Mary said, "from last year."

There was a pause.

"Pigeons-in-a-blanket!" I said.

People stared.

"I mean pigs," I corrected.

"Pigs-in-a-blanket?" Li said. "Excellent choice."

Pigs-in-a-blanket had been the smash hit of our Christmas party sixteen months before. The name, as much as the food, had delighted guests, including Li Feigan. Better known as sausage rolls, the dish was easily prepared: meat from a local market, imported butter, flour, water. This evening we would offer pigs-in-a-blanket with sides of pasta and salad—another mongrel menu, interbred out of necessity.

"We thought about cows," I said, "but decided they were too fat. And sheep don't need blankets; they've already got wool sweaters."

People sipped drinks.

"That was a joke," I thought to add.

All eyes fell on the fabled main dish. Though the sausage was tasteless, Mary's crust was buttery and sweet. Yu Wei, who had not attended the Christmas party, inspected the delicacy, took a bite, then grimaced down at her feet.

"In Xidan Street many years ago," she offered, "a jiao zi vendor was arrested for using strange meat in his dumplings."

"Oh?"

"Officials discovered human flesh in the filling."

I stopped chewing.

"The *jiao zi* were filled with human meat," Wei continued, holding the sausage roll at arm's length. "The vendor was accused of—"

"Rumors!" Li interrupted, his mouth full. "No one can verify this."

"People are quite sure of which shop in Xidan," Wei said.

"Which people?"

"Beijing people."

"*Which* Beijing people?" he insisted.

Flushing, Yu Wei mumbled in her own language that *lao bai xing* agreed the story was true. Her citing of "ordinary people" was telltale. Actually, *laobaixing* translated as "the old hundred names," a reference to the fact that three-quarters of the country shared a single directory page of surnames: Zhao, Qin, Sun, Li, Zhou, Wu, Zheng, Wang, Liu, Zhang and so on. These appellations were venerable and ancient; it was not uncommon for a friend to trace ancestors back twenty generations. Emperors, generals, poets, painters, even outlaws and counter-revolutionaries shared monikers with farmers and factory workers and folks who swept the streets. A student might have been born in 1969, but his name, his place in the cosmos, was older than the most ancient temple, the knobbiest tree. Membership in *laobaixing* expanded that cosmos immeasurably. Suddenly an individual was connected to strangers who had lived eight centuries ago, or who were living now in a city two thousand kilometers away. Suddenly Deng Xiaoping and Wei Jingsheng were vaguely related, part of the same community. That dictators and their victims shared family names, shared them not only with each other but with the so-called masses and therefore were all "ordinary people," was a startling thought, curiously difficult to digest. It was, to say the least, a fractious clan.

Li Feigan, however, was not buying *laobaixing*'s opinion of Xidan Street dumplings. "Nonsense," he said, waving Yu Wei's conjecture into the air.

Wei reddened further.

"The spaghetti sauce has only onions and tomato," I said, swallowing a bite of sausage roll with difficulty. "Would someone pass it to me?"

The conversation strayed, mercifully, from gastronomical tall tales. First we discussed our wall hanging and decided, as always, that the sheet of calligraphy was either extremely ancient, extremely illegible or, as Li Feigan obstinately insisted, the work of a foreigner ill trained in the art. My theory that the calligraphy was both the writing on the wall, as Zhao Zhenkai had suggested, and a kind of Rorschach test of cultural inclinations met with stony silence. Li was even more adamant than usual that the work was a forgery.

"I am very busy these days," he said, to explain his sour mood. "Researching my thesis, looking for a job and also dealing with the problem of housing."

I inquired.

"I would like the school to provide me a room for next year," he answered. "To find a job in Beijing, I will need to be able to prove that I have accommodation."

"Is the school willing to give you a room?"

"It is strictly against the rules."

"Are the rules breakable?"

"There is no need to break them," Li said. "Only to make an exception."

"What about a residency card for Beijing?" Mary asked.

"Also an exception."

"Li is famous," Houxing repeated.

He ignored the gibe. "Problems are problems only because no one has solved them," he said rather cryptically.

"Gifts?" I suggested.

"Not necessary in my case. I am owed favors. I have done extra work for the college administration. I have good *guanxi* here."

"What about the job?"

"The job is different," he admitted. Then, tugging at the cuffs of his shirt, Li clasped both arms of the chair. "To locate employment in the capital without a residency card is challenging. For most students the situation is hopeless. The government does not want people to remain in the city. Beijing is too crowded, with not enough jobs to satisfy the peasants who come here, hopeful but uneducated. People should stay in their hometowns and help make those places prosperous."

Mary nodded. Houxing ate her sausage roll. Yu Wei sulked over a glass of Coke. I spoke up. "So you are content to return to Jining after graduation?"

Li's smile broadened. "Jining is a provincial village," he said patiently. "There is nothing there for a person like me. I will find a job in Beijing and arrange to live at the college for a year, until Houxing has completed her degree."

"You *must* be famous," I said.

He took no notice of my quip either. "I have invited several people to a dinner party next week. A man who is a friend of my father has a senior position in the government. He likes the Western-style restaurant in the Beijing Hotel."

"You've invited him to the Beijing Hotel?"

"He is an important connection."

"Do they take—?"

"I need to exchange some *renminbi* for FEC," Li added, lowering his gaze. "The restaurant accepts only Foreign Exchange Certificates."

"Even from nationals?"

"Three hundred *yuan* should be enough."

Li Feigan needed three hundred *yuan*, or four months' living expenses, to purchase on the black market sufficient funny money—like the regular currency, FEC was nonnegotiable—to buy favors from mandarins. These men apparently delighted in insisting the ambitious peon stand them dinner in the shabby state-run restaurant in the shabby state-owned Beijing Hotel, an establishment that overcharged with impunity because it was so famous, so central (just off Tiananmen Square), and for decades was the only place where foreign tourists could stay. Once inside the block-long edifice, Li would be expected to smile gratefully as the cadre, along with a few tag-along cronies, ordered the most expensive dishes on the menu, guzzled Qingdao beers and Cokes, and then commandeered a one-hundred-*yuan* bottle of *mao tai* liquor to commence the endless, and increasingly inebriated, toasts and compliments and finger-counting games. The *mao tai* would be added to Li's bill, of course, payable exclusively in a half-baked currency that he could go to jail for even possessing.

"I'll look after the exchange for you," I said quietly. Li nodded, eyes still lowered. Silence collapsed the room. Conversations had been imploding with such swiftness lately that it was impossible to predict their demise. Unprepared, I scrambled for a new topic, and found it in a side dish. "When I was a kid," I began, "we would make shapes out of strands of spaghetti. Countries, for example, or human faces."

Everyone, including Mary, stared at me. I pressed on. "We could, let's see, try and shape our home provinces. Separate one or two strands of pasta and then move them around the plate with your fork ..."

Houxing went first. She sculpted Shandong province with a single spaghetti strand. While Yu Wei fiddled with her fork and Li folded his arms in dissent, Mary created an outline in tomato sauce.

"Where is this?" Houxing asked her.

"Wisconsin."

Houxing smiled. Li did not.

"What about you, Wei?" I said.

Yu Wei lowered her fork. "I cannot work with the materials," she sighed.

I had to act fast. "Here's mine," I said, angling my plate for display.

"Ontario?" Li said, his knowledge of geography impressive.

"Not Canada," I answered. "A local country."

"But you said—?"

"Never mind what I said."

"Australia?" Wei offered.

"Closer."

"Afghanistan?" Houxing tried.

"Even closer."

"Mongolia?" Mary said.

The suspense was killing them.

"Tibet," I said, taking pity.

Our guests leaned forward to examine the three-strand outline. "Very nice," Houxing said. —

"Tibet is not so large," Li protested.

I shrugged.

"Tibet is also not a country."

"We'll eat it anyway," I said, clearing the table. Li immediately donned his humble waiter hat, plates stacked in one hand, glasses in another, with a slight bow in Mary's honor. In the kitchen his expression hardened.

"Tibet has always been part of the nation," he said in a low voice.

"Hu Yaobang," I replied.

"The anniversary of his death ... I know this."

"He visited Tibet in 1980."

"His trip was well reported," Li admitted. Knowing what was coming, he retired the smile.

"Hu described Beijing's presence in Tibet as 'pure colonialism,'" I said. "How can you colonize your own country?"

"Mistakes were—"

"How?"

Li wanted to argue, but was probably under pressure from Houxing to be gracious. I wanted to argue, but was supposed to be hosting a party. We settled on gibes.

"Westerners cannot understand the situation," he said.

"Westerners cannot accept the situation."

"It is an internal matter."

"It is an international concern."

"We have done much—"

"What you are doing is—"

Houxing joined us. "Can I help?" she asked.

"Li is giving me a recipe for pigeon *jiao zi*," I said. "He recommends using only Asian Games birds."

Houxing's hearty laugh forced Li to grin once again. But then, in the living room, he gently took my arm.

"Hu Yaobang is greatly missed," he said. "He was a sensible man. With Zhao in disgrace, the current leaders are not ... "

We sat down.

"...adequate," Li said, completing his sentence.

"Who do you mean?"

He hesitated.

"Isn't Deng retired?" I said.

Li looked first at his wife, then at me. "Perhaps it is not appropriate," he said.

"Politics," Wei shuddered.

"Very depressing," Houxing agreed.

"Did any of you hear that Chai Ling and her husband escaped to Hong Kong last week?" I persisted.

"Yes," Houxing said. "We heard."

There was another pause. Finally Mary turned to Li. "Do you know Zhou Shuren very well?" she said.

"Only a little."

"He is a *liu-mang*," Yu Wei mumbled.

"Does he have a brother?"

"A brother?" Li replied. "I am not so close to him to say. But it is possible."

Typically, no one asked Mary why she was inquiring about Zhou Shuren. Li did, however, add a thought. "He left campus two weeks ago without informing the English department. A friend in the faculty had to take over his classes."

"He didn't tell Dean Shen?"

"A phone call," Li said, "several days afterward. The dean was very angry. He is telling people that Zhou Shuren is a wildcat who will end up badly. Dean Shen is not counting on him for the future."

Yu Wei tut-tutted such a character. Oddly, the conversation shifted briefly to Wei's sailor husband, who was recently on furlough in Beijing. Though the man's request for a transfer to the capital to be with his wife had been rejected, he was reassured by superiors that another application five or ten years hence might meet with more favor. Wei appeared thoroughly resigned to the wait.

At the door, she pulled me aside, checking that Li was out of earshot. "There is proof that the vendor used human meat in the *jiao zi*," she whispered, fanning her hand across her mouth. "The story is told all over the city. People who ate the dumplings got sick."

"*Laobaixing?*" I asked.

"Some died," she nodded. "The man was sent to prison for twenty years."

"Incredible," I said.

For three days afterward, Mary and I ate leftover pigs-in-blankets. Each evening, gazing at the sallow nubs of sausage that poked out from the pastry shells, we debated the virtues of vegetarianism and agreed that under no circumstances would the Xidan Street dumpling stalls get our business.

Rumors were terrible things.

Li Feigan's political entanglements deepened the next week. The issue now was basketball. As part of the "Forget 1989" campaign, the administration had cajoled the physical-education department into organizing a series of sports tournaments. The staff basketball competition, scheduled for the final days in April, was a major event, especially when it was announced that participation by department members was at the discretion of each dean. The tournament coordinator also agreed that foreigners who taught in the departments were entitled to participate. Though unwelcome at staff meetings and uninvited to faculty outings, both Mary and I could play basketball for Dean Shen. Similarily, an American whose department had once been under the English umbrella was eligible to play with us. The American was six foot two and had a decent outside shot. Just when it began to look as if English the language and English the faculty were indeed trying to take over the world, Li Feigan compounded the insult by declaring *himself* eligible, based on his part-time teaching post with the institute's continuing education branch. Not only were his criteria suspect, but Li would also be betraying his own colleagues—a hapless bunch of graduate students—to wallow in the foreigner-tainted hegemony of the English team.

Dean Shen was behind Li's decision. The dean wanted to thrash the rival department, thrash every other department, to reestablish the ascendancy of a faculty battered by defecting professors, plunging student scores and a chief who might be dismissed from his post at any moment. Basketball would permit Shen Yanbing to remind fellow deans in the German and French departments that among international languages, English and only English could produce two strapping foreigners, all elbows and knees and spindly fingers, who, though ugly as calves, would stuff shots, scoop rebounds, set brick-wall picks and score, score, score.

The American and I were oblivious to this subtext until we arrived at the court on game day. Li Feigan had neglected to mention his maneuverings, and Dean Shen had outlined his bloody plan at a faculty meeting closed to foreigners. I had half suspected the department would be unable to field a squad. Not so. At three o'clock on April 26, a brooding afternoon, the sky cinereous with dust, fifteen staff assembled below a basket to bum cigarettes, exchange gossip and shoot the odd warm-up shot. Of the fifteen, three were in their "golden years," includ-ing the ancient assistant dean, Madame Sun; six had clearly not touched a basketball in decades; eight wore pants and hard-soled shoes; and nine were complete strangers. This phantom faculty (the English department was rumored to employ over one hundred teachers, half of whom were currently "inactive") ignored us, chattering with friends and sipping the sodas designated for the break. When the referee blew his whistle, however, the ghosts ambled from the court: the majority wan-dered back to their apartments before the game even started. That left six players, Coach Shen and an audience of bored teachers and bemused undergraduates. With the sky darkening and the air suddenly standing still, it seemed wise to hasten the proceedings.

The opposition squad, composed of technical staff, fired the first salvo. The English team was stacked, they complained, rife with scabs and hired guns. I was an known entity. But what about the sandy-haired American? And Li Feigan—wasn't he a graduate student? Dean Shen went berserk. How dared a bunch of mechanics and video repairmen question his department! What did they know about the composition of a university faculty? Let the game begin, the dean announced with a sweep of his cigarette.

The opposition demanded a meeting with the tournament orga-nizers, refusing to start until their grievances were heard. Li Feigan, in turn, refused to answer any questions until after the match, preferably after the tournament. Dean Shen called the other team names. I did not understand all the abuse—Li was too engrossed to translate—and

I eventually retired to the stands to drink a soda and watch the dust swirl across the pavement. A half hour later, with two official protests lodged—one against our squad, the other in protest against the first protest—the referee finally ordered athletes into their positions. The game commenced with a bump and descended into a brawl. Resentful at our presence and furious at the dean's condescension, the technical department played murderously, venting unplumbed depths of frustration with their shoulders and elbows. It was no fun out there, but the dean refused to spell either foreigner, commanding us to block more shots and score more baskets. The air, meanwhile, began to clot, and the sky took on the yellow of dried cornstalks. When the wind rose, shifting skeins of dust over the court and unmooring the backboards, it was time to call it quits. The whistle sounded, and I was relieved. It turned out, however, to be only the break.

The teams argued away the intermission. Voices were raised and threats exchanged. Declining conditions (we were, in effect, in the middle of another dust storm) had dispersed most of the crowd, but nothing deterred the fanatics and their flunkies (the American and me). With visibility narrowed to a corridor of stinging light, and with gusts altering the arcs of shots, the second half deteriorate further into a violent comedy of errors. When it was over, the other squad refused to shake our hands, for which an ebullient Dean Shen taunted them, dancing around their huddle like a bully looking for a fight. Head pounding from inhaling too much animosity, I left quietly, abandoning a scene that resembled the floor of a political convention after a divisive final vote.

Next morning, the anniversary of the April 27 march on Tiananmen Square, the English department was stripped of its victory for using ineligible players. Shen Yanbing called an emergency meeting to formulate a strategy. The faculty withdrew from the tournament and the dean stormed the college president's office to protest the insult. Li Feigan's machinations, intended to ensure Dean Shen's support of his housing ruse, backfired: the dean accused Li of bungling the affair, causing him to lose even more face on campus. Bewildered, Li tried to rejoin his proper squad, but his fellow graduate students also protested and also withdrew. Next, the American was told that his tiny department *was* going to field a team, now that the English faculty was out of the competition. When the squad arrived for its first game, however, the opposition—a vengeful gang of technicians—protested that the American was moonlighting and refused to play. The technical department forfeited the match and a day later also quit in protest.

As the tournament lurched toward its conclusion, I kept turning up at the games scheduled for my faculty, and usually managed to assemble four or five friends and undergraduates. Let's play anyway, I would offer the opposition squad leader. Once it was established that the English department had indeed forfeited the match, the other team would pose a question: Why bother, if they'd already won? For fun, I would answer. That was hilarious. For fun? Amusement, I elaborated. Relaxation. Sometimes the team would convene a meeting, decide that I was merely eccentric and agree to a friendly game. But most often the opposition guffawed at my suggestion and retired from the court. Colleagues in the English department, meanwhile, including a few of the teachers I had encountered for the first time during warmups, approached me in the office or along pathways to denounce my grandstanding. Didn't I realize that by continuing to participate in the competition I was insulting Dean Shen? The dean had lost face, the department had lost face—how could I be so crass?

The tournament championship consisted of a match between two of the four teams (out of an original dozen) that had not withdrawn in protest or dissolved from lack of interest. The game was played on May 4.

3

DING LUOJIN

L uojin wanted to cook for us: dishes from her home province, foods her mother prepared on holidays. For her, the exercise would be a way of forgetting, or remembering in a different way. Ding Luojin wanted to obliterate all but the most lighthearted images of her own family gatherings. It was May 6, and she had just been informed of her job assignment: as expected, she would in future be a translator for a travel agency in a town where no one traveled or spoke foreign languages. The position was for life, and the work unit the travel agency was attached to would soon receive her file, a secret record of Luojin's trespasses, and would subsequently issue her fresh sets of cards—city, unit, medical—and demand that the old ones be handed over and destroyed so that her existence in Beijing could be officially erased. She would not be briefed during this process, nor welcomed into the smoky meetings of administrators and deans and other demigods to receive their wisdom. Last spring there had been talk of allowing students to choose their own jobs, but the Turmoil had snuffed out that reformist heresy. The current buzzword was "grass-roots," a 1990 euphemism for a Cultural Revolution punishment: banishing pesky scholars to rural backwaters, where the exigencies of survival—finding enough food and a place to sleep, learning how not to antagonize locals—would quell more fervent thoughts. The majority of the senior class could look forward to being assigned to a grass-roots work unit for a year, or two, or three, and by these standards Luojin's placement, back in her hometown, where she could stagnate on a full stomach, rot in a warm bed, seemed relatively tolerable. Luojin, however, considered the position a death sentence, and not having heard since February from the relative with the connection in Shenzhen, she was in despair. "I cannot survive in reality," she explained.

We were in the kitchen. Luojin smiled bravely, and tucked strands of hair behind her ears. Then, picking up a cleaver, she massacred the vegetables on the cutting board. "What is there left to be happy about?" she asked above the staccato of her own chopping.

"How about novels?" Mary said.

"Novels no longer work. Now we find only sad stories with unhappy endings. It is too difficult to read these books. They remind us of us." She giggled, near tears.

"What about movies?"

"Since Mr. Zhou went away, there have not been many movies. He chose good movies from America, full of bad things we shouldn't watch. Now the department shows us boring movies full of good things we should watch.

"Many students have become interested in religion," Luojin continued, still chopping. "They are borrowing books on Western religions from the library. Also, there are foreign teachers who wish to talk with us about these things."

"They're called 'born-again Christians,'" I said. Shortages of foreign teachers after June 4 had smoothed the way for missionaries—mostly Southern Baptists from the United States but also evangelical Catholics, Protestants, even a Mormon—to fill the vacancies.

"They use those words," Luojin agreed.

"'Born-again'?"

"Yes."

"Do you visit these teachers frequently?"

"Only one time. They offered Cokes and American chocolates, and were very nice. But I am not so interested in their religion."

"What about your friends?"

"Some visit more often. But I would like to find a God for myself. A nice God, for a change." She paused, the cleaver suspended in the air. "My parents believed the Communist Party was God, and Chairman Mao. We had pictures of Mao on the walls of our apartment, and a shrine to him in the main room, which my father and mother prayed to every morning when I was a baby. Yet my parents are intellectuals! Isn't that strange? Now, of course, we have nothing. We have nothing and believe in nothing also. How can we live this way?"

Luojin's habit of posing ponderous questions in the most matter-of-fact voice, as though she were asking about the weather, could be disconcerting. We had learned long ago to treat the inquiries as rhetorical. Still, I decided to respond.

"Maybe people need a rest from Gods," I said.

She ordered me aside to reach the stove. Though businesslike in the kitchen, Luojin still stopped to consider: "It depends on the God," she said simply.

Fearing the bite of an oil-spitting wok, Mary and I retreated into the dining area. Luojin fired in the diced vegetables and in five minutes she had stir-fried an eggplant in garlic, a curried chicken dish, some lentils and added fresh grease patterns to the back wall of the kitchen. We admired the food and complimented the chef.

"Looks good," I said.

"As tasty as your mother would make?" Luojin asked.

"Easily."

"Wonderful!"

A fan of Coke, Luojin guzzled a glass before taking a bite of lunch. When I rose to offer her more, she beamed in gratitude, proffering a compliment that she had been holding in reserve.

"Your humor in class this morning was very ... humorous," she said.

"The joke didn't work," I apologized.

"The student Bei Hua explained it to us afterward. It took several minutes to understand the meaning. But then we all laughed."

"I probably shouldn't have bothered," I said. "It's a cultural thing." Actually, the joke, concerning a talking dog that could only say *ruff! ruff!*, had bombed partly because of linguistic differences over the sound a dog makes, but mostly on account of my miserable technique as a comedian.

"Bei Hua is very knowledgeable of foreign cultures," Luojin said. "He is maybe half-foreign himself." She offered the assessment thoughtfully, without rancor. Chopsticks pressed to her lips, she smiled dreamily, and for a second I imagined it was in fond memory of my joke. "Hua is getting into trouble again," she mentioned. "His thesis is concerned with the Turmoil."

That morning, Bei Hua, still awaiting the administration's decision, had revealed to me his intention of writing his senior thesis on local media coverage during the student movement. A more politically incorrect subject would be hard to imagine.

"It seems crazy," I concurred.

"He does not care. As well, Hua doubts the administration will expel him so close to graduation."

"What do you think?"

"I am too scared to think."

"But what do you think about Bei Hua?"

She sighed. "I like listening to him talk. He is very brave, and reminds me of last year. But," Luojin added after a pause, "I am also afraid of Bei Hua. I do not *want* to be reminded of last year. It was a terrible mistake. Students did not understand the implications of our actions. We were misled."

"By outside influences?"

"Possibly."

Despressed, we ate in silence.

"It is hopeless," Luojin said, poking the chicken with her chopsticks. "Students are so weak and the government is so strong and cruel. Bei Hua should leave the country. I should leave the country, to Shenzhen, where I can earn money and be alone."

"Do most undergraduates feel the movement was a mistake?" I asked, dreading her answer.

"We are not sure. It has hurt us. Things are worse now than before. And we were influenced by strangers to act in a manner that was outside normal behavior. Now our lives will be terrible, won't they?"

Mary had heard enough. "Do students really miss Mr. Zhou?" she asked suddenly.

"Oh yes," Loujin replied. "He is among our favorite teachers. Will he be gone much longer?"

It had been a month since Zhou Shuren's disappearance, and the English department had so far failed to track him down. Those colleagues not indifferent to his fate were beginning to express concern. Going unaccounted for, even in such a vast country, wasn't easy; strange faces in neighborhoods were routinely questioned by *lianhefangwei* patrols. After a point, absences were treated as defections into the reportedly burgeoning underground of criminals, political fugitives and ordinary people fed up with work-unit shackles. Zhou was fast approaching that point.

"We hope not," Mary said. "Did Mr. Zhou ever mention his family in class?"

Luojin shook her head.

"He has a brother, doesn't he? A brother who is ill?"

"His family is from Qinghai. Some people say they are not Han. This explains Mr. Zhou's bad behavior. He is a hooligan," Luojin said breezily.

"The students think Mr. Zhou is a *liu-mang*?"

"Of course! He wears old clothes and sometimes smells of beer. Also, his hair is long and he likes to use bad English words in class."

"Aren't you afraid of having a hooligan as a teacher?" I said. "In the city, *liu-mang* commit crimes and hang around bars late at night."

"Mr. Zhou is different. He is educated."

"Is he a 'we'?" I inquired.

Mary glared at me. Happily, Ding Luojin didn't understand my meaning. "Mr. Zhou and Miss Zhang are my favorite teachers," she said. "If I could be any person, it would be Miss Zhang."

"Why her?" Mary asked. Though Zhang Naiying remained Mary's closest friend at the college, they saw each other infrequently. In the middle of a second national tour with Taiwanese tourists, Naiying was sending us letters every week on the stationeries of international hotels in Shanghai, Guilin and Guangzhou that would normally have barred her from their lobbies. Zhang Naiying had now tried twice to resign from the English department. Twice Dean Shen had commuted the resignation into a leave of absence, thus delaying yet another staff departure.

"She is beautiful," Luojin offered, "and popular with men. Her English sounds very American, and she has many Western friends. As well, Miss Zhang is a tour guide. She earns foreign currency."

"Did she tell you this?"

"She has not taught us in months. But everyone knows."

"Knows what?"

"That she is paid by the Taiwanese in FEC or American dollars. And that the teacher Mr. Zhai is in love with her. He is handsome, but speaks too British. We like romances very much, and teachers who have American accents."

"But don't teach ..." I said.

"Teaching pays poorly," Luojin explained. "Also teachers are not respected in the society. Why would a person want to teach?"

Luojin had an afternoon class in Marxism, which was more likely another reeducation session on the Turmoil, where she would ingest more rote expressions like those she had offered us in translation. She hastily polished off the leftovers and finished the Coke.

"Thank you for letting me cook," she said at the door. "And, forget. You are definitely my favorite foreign teachers."

"We're your only foreign teachers," Mary said.

"I know!"

I had to settle something in my mind. "Could you imitate a dog for me?" I asked.

"What?" Mary said.

"*Wang! wang!*" Luojin said, flushing.

"A dog says *wang*?"

"Of course."

"Not *ruff! ruff!?*"

She howled with laughter.

"Go, Luojin," Mary commanded, pushing her into the corridor. "You don't want to be late for Marxism."

Shu Sheyu congratulated me the next evening for being famous on campus.

"Famous for what?" I asked.

"Your strange jokes," he answered, "and animal imitations." "Only one animal imitation," I corrected. "And it didn't work. In fact, it was a disaster. Why would this make me famous?"

Shu was amused. *"Because* the animal imitation was so terrible," he said. "Also because you repeated the joke twice."

"I was hoping it would improve," I admitted. "I thought if I told the joke better, my students would laugh the second time."

"Did they?"

"A little. But at me, not the humor."

We were on the track. Shu rarely did laps—they aggravated his limp—and he hated the rain. I had begun to appreciate walking in a circle and had also developed a taste for "natural" Beijing spring weather: bruised skies, translucent mists, a pollution haze that dulled even the brightest sunlight. My presence on the sports ground was, therefore, within character. What about Shu? Not only did I encounter him walking in a twilight shower, but he was limping along, baseball cap on his head, book in hand, reading. Startled, I hesitated to intrude. Shu noticed me.

"Isn't it hard to read while walking?" I asked.

"Not so hard,"

"And in the dark?"

"There is still some light," he said.

"And in the rain?"

"The rain is okay," he decided.

We were silent for a minute. "What are you doing out here, Shu?" I finally asked.

"Walking around the track. Tonight I will do twenty-six circles, one circle for each day leading up to the anniversary of June 4."

"Leading *down* to the anniversary, you mean," I said. "You're counting backward."

"I suppose," he agreed. "On June 4 I will need to make only one circle to complete the punishment."

"Punishment for what?"

Shu only shrugged.

"When did you start?" I continued.

"April 27. The date of the—"

"Yes," I interrupted. "What will you do after you complete the final lap?"

Shu blinked his eyes in contemplation. "Maybe I will get arrested on Tiananmen Square," he said. "Maybe I will resign from the university. Maybe," he concluded, breaking into a crooked smile, "I will do nothing, like everyone else."

He spoke the words blithely. Everything to Shu Sheyu was funny, and not funny; little was worth fretting over.

"What are you reading?" I inquired.

He turned the book over in his hands. "Lao She's short stories.* Written before Liberation, before the Red Guards drowned him in a lake outside Beijing."

"Is that what happened?"

"Naturally," Shu replied. "He was a great writer and a patriot. What else would the Red Guards have done with him?" His tone was still breezy, but now there was a chill.

"How's Cathy these days?" I tried. When he looked at me blankly, I added, "The track-and-field star? One- and two-hundred meters, and the long jump?" Grimacing, Shu stared down at the book, fanning the pages with his fingers. "Some night, huh?" I said hastily. "Less than perfect for outdoor penance."

*Lao She (1899–1966) was a popular Beijing writer, best known for the novel *Rickshaw*. Persecuted during the Cultural Revolution, he died under mysterious circumstances.

He did not answer.

I asked how many laps remained.

"Thirteen," Shu said.

"But that will take another hour."

Shrugging again, he made a suggestion. "Why don't you tell me your animal joke?" he said.

"No thanks."

"I would like to laugh about something," Shu confessed.

"But the joke's not funny," I pointed out. "Remember?"

Eager to change subjects, I reminded Shu of a promise he once made, inspired by his reading of Zbigniew Brzezinski, to explain to me how things worked here, and why there was little hope. "Why don't you explain your theory?" I said.

"No thanks," he answered.

"It would pass the time?"

"An hour would not be nearly enough," he said gruffly.

Shu waved me home. Ten seconds later he called my name from across the field, his voice a foghorn in a deepening night.

"What is 'penance'?" he asked.

"Pardon?"

"You used the word 'penance'—what does it mean?"

"An act performed in punishment," I answered, startled by how clearly my own voice carried.

"Punishment for what?"

"A sin that probably wasn't your fault," I said.

"A sin?"

"Mistake."

"A mistake beyond your control?"

"Something like that."

He was silent. I squinted into the darkness, but it was hopeless.

"Naturally," Shu Sheyu said.

4

SHU SHEYU

The rumor slithered from gossip to gossip like a slug across a rock. I was let in on it twice in one day, and though the date was auspicious—the anniversary of the imposition of martial law, May 20—and a flurry of international incidents was filling the airwaves (including reports of negotiations to grant astrophysicist Fang Lizhi and his wife safe passage out of the country and the junking of the *Goddess of Democracy* ship in Taiwan to pay off debts), campus scuttlebutt was focused on a local scandal. Did you hear, people began, that the track-and-field star— Knowing what was coming, I cut them off. I don't *want* to hear, I said. Did you hear, they insisted, that Li Wei, self-styled feminist and freethinker, just up and—I am deaf, I interrupted. No use telling me anything. She just up and dumped—Don't! I pleaded. Dumped him because of his—His what? I said. Tremendous intelligence? Original character?

"Li Wei has ended it," Shu offered at the door that evening. "We will no longer date each other."

"I'm sorry."

"She apologized for not wanting to see me."

I nodded.

"It was because of our different ages. Also, she has a boyfriend in her hometown." Shu paused, still in the doorway. "He is a high-jump star," he said.

"Do you want to come in?"

"Very tall man," he added vaguely. "Tall and muscular. They train together in summers, and will represent their province in national competitions."

"We have beer," I said.

"Bourbon?"

Shu poured himself a glass of bourbon. "Martial law began today," he said. "It is good to get drunk."

Removing his jacket, he headed straight for the living room, stopped before the sheet of calligraphy, seemed to examine it, then shook his head and switched on the television. The American drama "Beauty and the Beast" had just started, and Shu dropped into a chair. I studied his profile. His face was vivid but pale, and his eyes, normally so clear they seemed transparent, were muddied. Sinking his chin into his hands, he stared at the screen with such intensity that it was obvious he wasn't seeing a thing. I asked him about the show.

"It is very popular these days," Shu explained. "People think the hairy man is interesting."

"'Beauty and the Beast' was an odd series to dub," Mary said. "It's not exactly representative of American life."

"I like the sewers," Shu admitted.

He translated some of the dialogue back into English for us. The program, based on the legend of the beautiful woman who recognizes the nobility of a deformed man but must struggle to overcome her physical revulsion, was decent television. Though the plot of the episode was banal, the show attempted to treat serious themes: unrequited love, loneliness, appearances versus reality. "Beauty and the Beast" also depicted a squalid New York where daylight was pallid and night was long with shadows; much of the action took place in the underground world of the city's sewer system. We watched this cheery fare for half an hour, commenting on the impressive makeup job that had transformed a handsome actor into a monster. "For an hour a week," Shu pointed out quietly.

Then it was time to cook. For months, Shu had been promising us a lesson in the rudiments of the cuisine, but previous dinners had been too festive for discussions of the boiling of bean curd or frying of fish. Tonight was certainly not festive—grains of sand rapped on the kitchen window, the wind cat-howled up the stairwell—nor busy, with fewer students dropping by to visit and more colleagues removing themselves from campus to seek other employment or, in Zhou Shuren's case (we surmised), pursue nihilism as a life-style. Shu, however, was also out of sorts, exuding an edginess at odds with his normally unflappable character. I tried to cheer him up.

"I've been reading *Outlaws of the Marsh*," I said, referring to the fourteenth-century Shandong epic of crime and adventure, "and I can't get over how many scenes involve eating and drinking. Everyone has 'tidbits' with wine before the meal, then dishes of meat, fish and vegetables, with dumplings afterward."

"We love food," Shu agreed.

"And the dishes seem similar to what people eat today. Imagine, to be eating the same food in 1990 as in the fourteenth century," I whistled in appreciation. "Continuous culture," I said. "Amazing."

"Think so?"

"Sure. Six hundred years later—same food, same appetites, same people."

"This is amazing?"

"I guess it is," I equivocated.

"A great achievement?" he continued. "The mark of an ancient civilization?" I looked at Shu, but he abandoned the thought. "I will need garlic," he said. "Also onions, and a sharp cleaver."

Shu's culinary skills were intuitive. For ninety minutes we observed him chop, dice and shred, mix spices and measure portions while rethinking, redesigning, often restarting a dish at the last moment, all without comment or instruction. Answers to our questions were perfunctory; he appeared to cook in a haze, unaware that he had pupils in the kitchen. Mary gave up, but I parked a chair near the door, withstanding blasts of vaporized oil and hissing soy. Only during the frying of spicy bean curd, when Shu plopped a dollop of chili sauce into the wok and an odor hit the air with the fury of gasoline, did I flee. The hallway was soon inundated with the smell and Mary and I retreated to the front balcony, where we could view our friend through the window, calmly stirring the concoction at the stove. We stayed outside for fifteen minutes. The gulf between Shu Sheyu and us was like the "fourth wall" in a theater: we were the audience, he, the actor on stage. Shu brightened to that idea and offered a soliloquy. The subject, for unexplained reasons, was Dean Shen.

"I have asked Shen Yanbing if I can teach a class in the English department," he began. "A course on Lu Xun in translation. Why not? No one understands what he is saying in the original, so perhaps his meanings will become clear in English? Dean Shen is a friend of mine. He will do this favor. He likes Zhou Shuren, and allowed him to return to the institute after his arrest, and now to disappear again without permission."

"Have you heard anything about Zhou?" I asked from the orchestra pit.

"People say he is in Tibet."

"Really?"

"Or Hong Kong, perhaps. He is not popular among teachers. It doesn't matter."

"Is his brother better now?" Mary said.

"What brother?"

"Zhou Shuren's brother—the one he went to visit?"

Shu guffawed. "If Dean Shen likes you," he said, "everything is okay. The undergraduate Bei Hua is being protected, and many others. Shen Yanbing is my friend also. He will not interfere in my private affairs. I am not in his department, do not attend his faculty meetings. During the basketball tournament I supported the English department when the organizers removed the victory from your team." Shu stopped to reoil the wok. What was he talking about? "Dean Shen could still lose his job. He was not made a full professor last month, and he is under terrible pressure to say terrible things. It is the anniversary of martial law this week, when the dean tried to retract his petition and deny that he had led the school onto Tiananmen Square. One year ago ..." he said to himself. "Not so long, for an ancient civilization."

The sentence gave us pause. "Next year you'll be in Denmark," Mary offered hopefully.

Shu shrugged.

"Drinking Danish beers," I added.

"Kissing Danish girls," he said blandly.

"How are the language classes going?"

"*Comme ci, comme ça,*" Shu answered.

Dinner was served. Though a cloud of chili-sauce vapors lingered near the ceiling, the sting had faded. Shu laid out a banquet: spicy bean curd, pork with egg, sautéed mushrooms and bamboo shoots, boiled meat balls, a sweet-and-sour fish. "To Li Wei," he said, raising a glass of beer. "A very nice girl."

"You know lots of nice women," Mary said.

"Naturally."

The food was delicious. Even the bean curd tasted mild. Still, we ate the meal in a heavy silence. The quiet extended beyond the apartment. Our building was sandwiched between two residences that boasted a combined population of six hundred, bodies squeezed between acoustically volatile cinder blocks. Yet tonight the edifices were mute, windowpanes reflecting the waning light.

"The campus seems kind of somber," I said.

"Boring," Shu corrected.

"Are people remembering?"

"People are leaving."

"Oh?"

"Teachers are looking for other jobs. Undergraduates are returning home until they receive their assignments. Attending classes serves no purpose. Teaching classes is also useless."

"I was hoping people were remembering," I said.

"No one is remembering. Everyone remembers. That is how things work."

We nodded.

"The most popular saying among students these days is from the movie *Hei Xue*," Shu continued.

"*Black Snow*," I translated.

"In the movie, the character played by Jiang Wen says something famous. '*Huozhe, mei jin. Si le, ye mei jin.*' It means, 'To go on living is boring. To die, however, is also boring.' But I have changed the expression a little."

"How?"

Shu stood up. Raising his left hand, he assumed a dramatic stance:

To be ... boring.
Not to be ... also boring."

He laughed, shook his head and disappeared into the kitchen for more beer.

Black Snow was the year's most controversial film, a bleak examination of contemporary urban life that was shot in Beijing during the winter of 1988–89, only weeks before the first student demonstrations. A man, Li Huiquan, played by the brilliant actor Jiang Wen, returns home after serving a prison sentence. During the interim his mother has died and his childhood sweetheart has gotten engaged. Numb and fatalistic, he becomes a free-market peddler in underwear, a career that exposes him to a world of shady characters and dubious activities. Materialism, meaningless sex, the realization of ambitions through thuggery and manipulation are the touchstones in this world, and the character succumbs to the vacant charms of the freewheeling 1980s, despite a growing sense of isolation, exacerbated by a failed romance with a heartless nightclub singer. The film's ending, in which the man is stabbed to death by *liu-mang*, is willfully absurd: a meaningless life expires stupidly.

Black Snow flatters neither Li Huiquan nor Beijing. The capital is cold and mercenary, ruthless in its distinction between those who count and those who don't. Though director Xie Fei was criticized for summoning ghosts in the socialist machine—prostitution, the black market, a growing pornography industry—his work escaped banning because it was deemed politically neutral. The film is actually a ferocious attack on a society that has been morally and spiritually emasculated. The good that does remain, evoked in brief scenes between neighbors in the crowded courtyard where Li Huiquan grew up, pales beside the hunger of a city to replace discredited human values with those of commerce and consumption.

Shu returned from the kitchen. "You'd make a good Hamlet," I said.

"Not Hamlet," he answered. "Richard III." Shu demonstrated: shoulders hunched, limp exaggerated, attitude malicious and clowning.

"But Richard III was a political animal," I said. "You hate politics."

"Everyone hates politics," he agreed.

"So Hamlet is better. He was reluctant, didn't really want to become involved."

He thought for a moment. "But Hamlet was noble," he said simply. "That is not possible for me."

The telephone saved us. Li Feigan needed to talk about his thesis for a few minutes: was it convenient? I invited him up, telling Shu to make himself coffee. Shu turned on the television instead, a glass of bourbon in his hand and a smirk on his face.

Li arrived and, refusing tea, launched into an explanation of why his thesis, until recently a guaranteed first honors, was suddenly in trouble. The paper, a study of translating classical poetry, was intelligent and well researched. It had come under fire from Dean Shen, who had demanded an unusual middraft reading of the manuscript and pronounced the work flawed. Since the basketball debacle, in fact, the dean had found Li Feigan wanting in every respect and had told him as much on several occasions, in public, without tact. Though Li had withstood the abuse silently, he was clearly humiliated and suffering under the strain. His collar was ringed in perspiration and his thoughts were strangely disheveled. Li's request that I reexamine the early chapters of the thesis to unearth the imperfections the dean had alluded to was an unprecedented confession of failure. I sought words of consolation. But Shu Sheyu, seated placidly across the coffee table, offered an unconsoling thought.

"You must regain the dean's support," he said, still smirking. "Perform more favors. Leave cigarettes on his table."

Li smiled back, gripping the armrests. "You do not understand the situation, Shu Sheyu," he said.

"I think I do."

"Gifts work only for students who hope to persuade the dean to give them a better job assignment," Li continued. "Or teachers who require the school's permission to study abroad."

"Don't be so sure," Shu said.

Li examined his knuckles. Then, glaring at Shu Sheyu, he delivered a knockout punch in his own language, speaking too rapidly for me to follow.

Shu stopped smirking.

"People say ..." Li added casually.

"They are wrong."

"Say what?" I asked.

"It is private," Shu snapped.

"Okay," I said.

Shu got up and left, not the room, the apartment, forgetting even his jacket. Mary emerged from the kitchen to ask what had happened, then followed Shu down the stairs.

Li Feigan stood as well. "The rumor is that Dean Shen ordered Shu's girlfriend to stop visiting him," he said.

"When?"

"Two weeks ago. The dean did not like an undergraduate going into a teacher's dormitory. Also, Li Wei is from an important family. The administration considered it improper for her to be ..." He let the sentence die. Wandering over to the calligraphy, Li chuckled at the incomprehensible ideographs, then stopped before the row of cassettes, a sure sign (he had little interest in music) that a speech was forthcoming.

"Today marks the first anniversary of martial law," he offered, the thesis rolled into a baton. "One year ago, the government announced it would end the Turmoil in Beijing."

"Yes," I said.

"Restore stability," Li added, tightening his grip on the papers. "Teach the students a lesson."

"I remember."

He examined some tapes. Then he flipped through a stack of magazines. Never had I seen Li Feigan struggle so visibly for words.

"A year ago today," I echoed.

"It seems a long time," he confessed.

"Really, Li? Even for an ancient civilization ...?" I said to anger him.

He smiled. "I have disturbed you enough. I will say goodnight."

I extended my hand.

"It is too bad about Shu Sheyu," Li said.

"What's too bad?"

"That he is a cripple ..."

"Don't forget to leave the thesis," I answered.

A hatred of politics was the most striking common feature among our friends. Regardless that many of them were naturally curious about the subject, and in another country might have become active in the political culture on some level, the fact remained that, as far as they could tell, politics in *their* country referred almost exclusively to the pursuit and maintenance of power. It was hard to disagree. If politics involved, as it did in certain nations, the process of governing, then, in a state where rule had always been an arbitrary prerogative notable for the suppression of any attempts to create process, lest these mechanisms interfere with personal agendas, power was the sole criterion for "successful" governance. If politics included the playing out of a compact between citizens and their officials, then, in a society where the citizen was free only to follow the four cardinal principles of socialism, free only to support the Party, free only to reject bourgeois liberalization and foreign influences and the pernicious teachings of Fang Lizhi, and where to inquire about a policy or to question an economic decision was treason, the compact was straightforward: it was not a compact at all. If a political culture was defined by the give and take, moderated through institutions and public forums, between individuals and the state, then, in a country where people counted as little more than tools of production and pawns in leadership struggles, and

where participation in civic affairs on a local basis consisted of regurgi-
tating the swill concocted in upper Party echelons, giving and taking
had about as much appeal as an extended visit to a reeducation camp.
It went on: the subjugation of a legal code to Party dictates, the reduc-
tion of the law court to a preamble to imprisonment or execution, the
abandoning of even modest reform in the wake of the overthrow of a
mandarin or a hiccup in factional squabbles. For Shu Sheyu and
others, politics was the means by which their lives were removed from
their control, so that days, months and years passed in quiet desperation and helplessness came to represent a habit of being, rather than a
lapse of energy.

But the citizen was not totally excluded from the procedure. The
aim of government propaganda was twofold. It sought to persuade
people to forget about those liberties they had never possessed, and
ideally never would. At the same time, however, propaganda also
encouraged the populace to denounce the ideas that underlay the liberties. If something had been suppressed, it must have been bad for the
country; if a reform was introduced from the outside, it must have
been malignant. The request was as incessant as it was absurd. Deeply
insecure about its legitimacy, yet determined to quash even the
faintest opposition, the Party leadership resorted again and again to
the most base and cynical of governing practices: turning individuals
against each other. Neighborhood watches, informants, public
denouncements, ideological and policy flip-flops that guaranteed even
the most patriotic would at some point be guilty of treasonous behavior—these served to inculcate servitude and internalize censorship to
such a degree that tanks and soldiers would be unnecessary except in
extreme circumstances, like June 1989. Declare it unlawful to think
and the majority of people would curb their thinking; declare debating
unpatriotic and the majority of people would cease to debate; declare
the imagination a threat to national stability and the imagination
would eventually be hunted down. The goal was to present citizens
with a cell—small, windowless, door ajar—and then manipulate,
indoctrinate and harass them until they entered the chamber without
prompting, clicking the lock shut behind themselves.

The same evening Shu Sheyu cooked for us, I lay in our living room listening for gunshots and tanks. Nothing had changed in four months; the echoes refused to fade, and the looming anniversary of June 4 only served to heighten the sounds that passed through my brain. I was bathed in sweat, drained from the humidity, and was at a loss to decide whether the serenity of the night—a crescent moon, chanting cicadas, curtains that gently swayed—disguised a menace. Closing my eyes, I confronted sandstorms and sirocco winds, mirages that shimmered on the horizon: images fueled by maps of empty quarters in Xinjiang and uncharted terrains in Western Tibet. After a while, I saw only a desert of black....

5

ZHOU SHUREN

"Hello?" called a voice from the corridor. "Anybody home?" I roused myself from the couch. Though it was late in the afternoon, the heat was oppressive and the pollen-clotted air seemed too thick to breathe. I had left the apartment door open to lure a draft up the stairwell.

"Zhou!" I said, rushing to shake his hand.

"You should lock your door," he said. "Keep out the bad elements."

"You're alive!"

"Am I?"

Zhou was better than alive: he looked tanned, rested, more muscular in the shoulders and arms. His hair was short and he wore a white T-shirt and green Bermuda shorts. Sunglasses nested in his hair and silver chains dangled from his wrists, like a Taiwanese pop star. The only glitch was the phrase emblazoned across the T-shirt in black letters: DOUBLE SUICIDE IS THE SUBLIME CULMINATION OF LOVE. I read the sentence twice.

"I bought the shirt from a girl on a train," he explained. "For six hours I sat in the seat across from her, studying the message. Something

173

told me it was meant for me. Finally the girl asked if I knew any English. When I said I did, she requested a translation of the words, which she had worn over her breasts for months without understanding them. I translated, and the girl started to cry. She sold me the shirt for ten *yuan*. Do you see her tears?" Zhou asked, indicating a faded stain.

"Wow," I said.

"I will never wash the shirt, in honor of that girl."

"What does it mean?" I had to ask.

"What does what mean?"

"'Double suicide is the sublime culmination of love'?"

"It means nothing," Zhou said.

"Oh."

"Like my life," he added unnecessarily.

"Which you cannot imagine without beer?"

He smiled. I took a bottle of beer from the fridge.

"Cold?" Zhou asked.

"Icy," I confirmed.

"I will never leave your apartment," he vowed.

He almost didn't. Handing back the cassettes he had borrowed eight weeks before, Zhou proceeded directly to the rear balcony, stopping only to punch at the curtains bunched into a corner of the room. The balcony was scorched, every inch raw to the sun, and afforded a blinkered view of a faculty apartment building, over-grown garden, coal-burning generator and in the distance, a tower on the neighboring campus where a graduate student had killed herself last October.

"The student left a note," Zhou said, visoring his eyes, "apologiz-ing to her family for sinking too deeply into the pit of bourgeois liber-alization."

"Did you know her?"

He shook his head. "She is dead, I am alive—how could I know her?"

"I meant—"

"Unless I am not alive, or else she is not dead. But you are certain that I am alive?"

"Pretty sure," I said.

"It is so hard to tell," Zhou sighed, pressing his glass to his cheek. "For one year I have done nothing. No one has done anything, but I have done less. Jumping off a tower would be something to do, you see. Jumping off a tower would be an activity."

"It's hot out here," I said.

"People are watching us," Zhou said, gazing across at the upper floors of the apartment building.

"How can you tell?"

"Because we cannot see them."

We retreated inside, drew the curtains across the windows (staff had recently rehung the drapes using stronger paperclips) and resettled on the narrow front balcony. It was leafy, smothered by an oak tree that climbed above the dormitory and harbored birds from the hunters, including cafeteria chefs, who roamed the path at dawn with rifles cradled in their arms. Foreigners grumbled about the wisdom of shooting into the trees, and sunbathed elsewhere. I transferred the cassette player into the kitchen, popped in Zhou's favorite tape—"War" by U2—and restocked the refrigerator with beer. Afternoon stretched lazily into evening, and Zhou Shuren drank, ate peanuts, etched shapes into the Gobi dust that powdered the balcony railing.

Mary returned shortly before dark. "It smells like a storm," she said from the hallway.

"Zhou's not alive," I answered.

She and Zhou hugged. "I ate twelve sparrows in Xidan Street last night, Mary," he said.

Mary stared at the T-shirt.

"Zhou is a full-fledged *liu-mang* now," I explained.

"How's your brother?" she asked.

"Much better."

"Has he recovered from his illness?"

"The illness is mental. He is sick in the head and maybe in the heart," Zhou said, flattening his palm over his chest as if to sing the national anthem. "There is no cure."

We retired outdoors.

"Have you been in Tibet all this time?" Mary wanted to know.

"Not Tibet," he replied. "Tianjin."

Tianjin was a sprawling port city 130 kilometers from Beijing. Though pleasant, it seemed an unlikely place for Zhou to have gone to exorcize his demons.

"What were you doing there?" Mary asked.

"I was looking for Atlantic City."

"And ...?"

"No luck," he answered with a shrug.

"Bad directions," I said.

"Actually," Zhou said, "I worked for five weeks shoveling coal into ships headed to Brazil. Ten hours a day, seven days a week."

We inquired.

"I needed the money to pay off a debt. Also to buy a video camera, or maybe to escape." He poured himself more beer. "Tianjin is an excellent city for bad elements. The black market is active and officials compete to take the biggest bribes. As well, the port of Tianjin is full of *liu-mang*, men who drink day and night, commit crimes, fight with knives and have sex with different women. They were my friends, and they protected me from *liu-mang* who were not my friends."

"Did you drink day and night?" I asked.

"Of course."

"Commit crimes?"

"One or two."

"Fight with knives?"

"We were at a disco one time, and I was dancing with a pretty girl. Some local men objected to the way I danced and wanted to beat me up."

"How do you dance?" Mary asked.

"I throw my body into other people," Zhou said, "to make contact, and also to destroy my mind. The men, who were not hooligans, complained that my dancing was too Western. They were planning to punch me until I bled. But then my *liu-mang* friends came over and showed their knives. The men left the disco quickly."

"Did you have sex with different women?" I wondered.

"I was not a *liu-mang* for very long," Zhou confessed, gulping his beer.

"Was it interesting being a hooligan?"

Forgetting his new trim, Zhou cleared his eyes of imaginary hair. "Sometimes," he answered.

"Do *liu-mang* read books?" I asked.

"Only *gong-fu* stories with sex and violence."

"Did you read them?"

"I tried. Too boring."

"What else do they do?"

"Nothing," he replied. "*Liu-mang* live without thinking, without caring. Everything is boring and stupid. It is a philosophy."

"Sounds bleak," I said.

"That's right," Zhou agreed. "But *liu-mang* also never lie. In order not to lie, they say little, you see, and fight with knives." He paused to drain his glass. "One night I told my hooligan friends about Tiananmen Square on June 4. I talked about seeing people die and hearing the sound of bullets fly through the air." Zhou offered the sound: *shwooh, shwooh.* "They got very angry with me."

"Why?"

"Because I was not killed by one of the bullets. I lived, which was a lie. I tried to explain that for me living was just a dream, but *liu-mang* do not like dreams."

We were silent.

"How is life in Beijing under martial law?" Zhou said, ignoring the past year.

"A lie," I answered.

"A dream," Mary said.

"You have been here too long," he said.

We were silent again. Rain had been falling for an hour. Drops flitted through the tree branches, causing leaves to shimmer and rustle, chant lullabies to the hiding birds. Though the sky was huge, it was also coal black; tendrils of electricity flickered across the upper margins. Zhou Shuren inverted a third bottle of beer into his glass and watched the foam surge over the rim, liquid pooling on the floor. He devoured a plate of spaghetti, plucked a leaf to wash his face and hands, then leaned over the railing to observe mortals scurrying for shelter below.

"Where are we?" he finally asked.

"The Middle Kingdom," I replied.

"It is perfect up here," Zhou said. "We can watch people, but they cannot watch us. We are safe. We are forgotten. Do I have to leave?"

"Stay, Zhou," Mary said.

"I cannot imagine my life without beer," he said passionately.

The thunder was low at first. Gathering fury, the final peal shattered the atmosphere. No bullet or even cannon could have matched such a repercussion, and we waited respectfully for the rumbling to fade. Zhou flinched at the thunder but yawned at the lightning that followed.

"What is the definition of a tank?" he asked.

We didn't know.

"The vehicle the PLA visits people in."

We smiled.

"What kind of cigarette does Li Peng smoke?"

We didn't know.

"Da ji."

Da ji, "Big Chicken": a cheap brand of cigarettes.

We laughed, kind of. Zhou spilled more beer. I made tea, which no one drank.

"Some people believe that thunder is God's anger," I said.

"Have I told you about the time I died in Tibet?" Zhou said.

"Yes."

"Should I tell it again?"

"Do you want to?"

He didn't answer.

"Tell us the story," Mary said.

Zhou slouched in the chair, erecting a steeple with his fingers. "Do you think God is in Tibet?" he wondered. Then, noting our hesitation, "That is a stupid question. I used to ask many stupid questions. Since the massacre I have stopped asking questions completely. Tonight I am feeling happy and drunk, and also was deceived by your apartment, and your big noses, into believing that this is not where it is and I am not who I am. As a result, I sank into the pit of bourgeois liberalization. I confess my crimes. But it is *your* fault that I asked about God, the fault of foreigners.... Do you have more beer?"

"That is a stupid question," I said.

"The girls at the Academy of Dramatic Arts are unbelievably stupid," Zhou offered.

"Zhou ..."

"But very, very pretty, Mary. Pretty and lively birds. They all laugh like this." Zhou covered his mouth with both hands and issued a stage twitter-giggle. He also rolled his eyes and batted his lashes, exactly like characters on the popular TV drama series. "Those girls will be big stars one day," he predicted.

"And they *all* laugh that way?" Mary said.

"That's right."

She stared at him. He drank. "Did you really eat twelve sparrows in Xidan Street yesterday?" she asked.

Zhou smiled feebly.

"You lied?"

"Forgive me."

"But that's good! Eating tiny birds is cruel."

"I wanted you to think I was a cruel man," Zhou said, his expression suddenly blank. "I wanted you to believe I was a genuine *liu-mang*."

The sky shattered again. The tremors multiplied gradually, paused for so long I thought they would subside, then released an explosion of such ferocity the campus expelled a gasp. For a moment, the storm was around us and the balcony was a balloon being hauled up through clouds, battered by wind and rain and bolts of lightning. Zhou Shuren stood to confront the maelstrom, beer glass in hand, and did what no one else we knew in Beijing had done before: he whooped. Loudly, arms raised, a grin glued to his face, Zhou hollered until he was hoarse. "I will never leave this apartment," he repeated.

"Stay, Zhou," Mary reiterated.

"Have I told you the story of the monk and his flower?"

"Tell us."

"The monk is being chased by soldiers of the Supreme Ruler, who has decided that all artists and people of learning must be executed, to make sure his supremacy is not questioned. The monk is not afraid of the People's Liberation Army, but is terrified of anyone who does what he is told." Zhou paused to search his thoughts. He emptied the glass. "So the monk comes to the edge of a cliff and begins to climb down it. The face of the cliff is steep, but the man is experienced at escaping. Above him are troops of the government. On the ground below, however, he sees an army of citizens with bricks and knives, waiting to capture him."

"An army of citizens?" I asked.

"Shh," Mary said.

"Citizens who will arrest the monk and bring him to the Party," Zhou said, shifting in his seat. "To prove their loyalty, and because they are extremely stupid. The monk even notices his brother in the mob, ready to betray his own family. So what should he do ...?"

The question was sincere, and we were pained to consider it. Our brooding was accompanied by faint aftershocks and slivers of light that still crackled in the air.

"He could eat the sweet flower he finds in a crevice?" I suggested.

"That's right," Zhou said. "Eat the sweet flower, and say fuck you to the army above and the army below. Fuck you to the chairman, and the Party, and the ..." He raised an empty bottle. "Do you have ...?"

I fetched the last beer.

"But the monk has no chance to eat the flower," he continued. "Before he can pick it, even open his mouth, *shwooh*, a bullet cuts through the air and kills him."

"Dead?"

"*Shwooh*," Zhou said, thrusting a finger into his heart to illustrate.

"Maybe God *is* in Tibet," I said.

"When I was in Lhasa, the city was full of stupid people," he offered. "Stupid soldiers and stupid cadres and tourists who wanted to climb mountains, not to die, or see God, but to take pictures and tell their friends about their adventures. Also, the beer was expensive."

His remark annoyed me. "What does the price of beer have to do with it?" I said.

"The bottles must travel by truck from Golmud, in Qinghai, down to Lhasa. The distance is great, and the roads in Tibet are bad."

"Where do you think Tibet is, Zhou?" I lectured. "On the moon? In North America? It's right—"

"The rain has stopped," Mary said.

"I cannot imagine my life—"

"Yes, yes," I interrupted.

"Maybe I will be able to imagine it in Tibet?"

"Of course," Mary said.

In the hallway, Zhou was suddenly transfixed by a swelling of the living room curtains. He crossed to the window and began beating the drapes, like a boxer with a punching bag. The act was so unexpected, and Zhou's face remained so impassive, that we both froze. Once he had finished, Zhou wobbled back to the door. We examined his T-shirt again, and he offered Mary a sodden retelling of the story.

"Are those the girl's tears?" she inquired, indicating fresh stains.

He pinched the shirt. "Those are new," he said. "Must be blood."

"Spaghetti sauce," I mumbled.

Zhou turned to me. "What are you rebelling against?" he asked abruptly.

"Me?"

"You."

"Nothing," I said.

He stared.

"What d'ya got?" I finally admitted.

I walked over to Zhou's building an hour later to apologize. The storm had cooled the air, and the campus seemed preternaturally still. A solitary street lamp transfixed a swarm of insects in its beam; I veered around the light, soaking my feet in shadowy puddles. Forced to grip the railing, I climbed to the third floor, which was darker than outside and reeked of urine. Zhou's door was shut but light crept under it. The roommate answered my third knock.

"Did I wake you?" I asked in his language.

"Zhou is asleep," the man replied in English.

"I'm sorry."

He was about to end the conversation when Zhou called out from behind the curtain that divided the room. Sighing, the roommate stepped aside. I drew the curtain. Zhou lay curled on the cot with his arms shielding his face and eyes. "I just wanted to drop these off," I said, holding out two cassettes. "I won't stay."

"I am very drunk," Zhou said in a hollow voice. "I was dreaming about Tibet."

"I should apologize—"

"It is my only dream these days," he added, from behind a web of fingers. "My only dream that is not stupid. Do you want to hear it?"

"Do you want to tell it?"

"Only if you have a dream also."

"I do," I admitted, not aware of the fact until that moment. "But is it, you know, wise?"

"Not wise," Zhou said.

I needed him to look up so I could gesture in the direction of the roommate on the other side of the partition. But Zhou remained enfolded in his own embrace, as if his useless consciousness were giving him a headache. To drown our conversaton, I grabbed a tape and slipped it into the machine. Though the cassette jacket had promised punchy rock and roll by The Pretenders, within seconds I became aware of a filing error: the music that flooded the room was elegant and elegaic, an evocation of ancient courtesies and forgotten sophistications. It was also traditional, compositions performed on a seventy-two-string harp called the *konghou*. The *konghou*, I remembered from the liner notes, had been popular in the Han and Tang dynasties (500–900), fell into disuse in the Ming Dynasty (1366–1644) and was then unheard for hundreds of years. In 1980, a group of scholars and craftsmen produced a copy of the instrument, eventually discovering manuscripts written for it. The musician was a young woman from Beijing.

"Shit," I said. "Wrong tape."

"It doesn't matter."

"I love the song titles on these traditional recordings," I said absently. "'Autumn Moon in the Han Palace,' or 'Regret of the Cowherd and the Girl Weaver.'"

"'Regret of the Cadre for his Little Red Book,'" Zhou offered.

"'Spring Blossom in the Factory Cesspool,'" I said.

"'Chairman Mao Gathers Manure and Orders His People to Eat It,'" he managed, gripping his head more tightly.

"Do you want something?" I asked in concern. "A glass of water? A beer?"

"Don't!" he laughed, writhing on the bed.

A voice startled us. "Beautiful music," the roommate called from his own cell. "For a change ..."

Zhou groaned. But the *konghou* was lovely, delicate and soothing. The counterpoint of harmonics with weeping notes, achieved by compressing a string, was unique to the instrument, as was its five-octave range.

"I'll go first," I said, hoping Zhou would sober up during the interval. "My dream is simple. Tibet is a country that isn't old, like here, isn't growing harsher all the time, isn't so exhausted. Because there are few people to age the land; there are only mountains and valleys, stupas and prayer flags. It's a place that is quiet, where the wind has a voice and the sky is vaulting, like a door onto eternity. It's a place where people are forever set against enormous landscapes," I continued, "set against those colossal, unchanging, eternal fixtures that lend human lives structure and permanence. People in this landscape are tiny, but not insignificant. They are alone, but not unhappy."

I stopped. What had I said? Already I could not remember exactly. Though the roommate coughed, Zhou lay perfectly still. I spoke his name. Getting no answer, I turned down the tape-player and sat at the foot of the bed. His breathing was labored but steady, and one arm had been lowered, exposing his profile. Zhou Shuren was thirty, but looked a decade younger; he wanted to die, but would probably survive another forty years. What would he do? How would he live? Eventually I rose and extinguished the lamp beside his head. Strains of *konghou* inflected my thoughts into the corridor and down the stairwell, long past the point where the music was actually audible.

Finding the south gate still open, I exited the campus and joined the main highway into the city. The road was pinched between regimental columns of trees and flanked by drumlins of watermelons stacked carefully by their owners, who slept on mats behind the mounds, in preparation for daybreak. The air now was ripe with night soil, a smell of growth and decay; a halo of flies hovered about my head. Street lamps, curled like candelabra, were ineffective, and the moon was fissured by branches and leaves. The occasional truck trundled past, still churning up dust despite the rain, and I shared the ditch with a stream of bicyclists whose passage through the night was processional, quietly dignified.

Outside the commerce institute, I checked the fence for a pair of bloody glasses—a weekly ritual—then squatted below the window of the shop that sold obscure machine parts. With my face cloaked, the few passersby no doubt took me for a drunk or a vagrant. The bullet holes were still there, of course, scars no physican knew how to heal. I fingered them. While the need was still private, it was no longer purely meditative; tonight I had to enumerate, to reassert objective realities through the listing of known truths, irrefutable facts. One year ago, minus forty-eight hours, thousands of unarmed people were massacred; on this very spot, a twenty-year-old commerce student was shot in the chest. Battles were fought in city streets; jeeps, trucks and buses burned out of control along this patch of road. Twelve months in the past, less two days, citizens of Beijing had declared this city their city, this country their country; in front of the machine-parts shop, next door to a restaurant, ten meters from an institute of higher learning, people had used bricks and bottles and finally their own bodies to impede tanks and troop carriers from advancing on Tiananmen Square. One year ago, along an undistinguished stretch of pavement in this suburban backwater, on the physical and psychological periphery of the capital, *something* happened. It had to have. Like *liumang*, bullet holes never lied.

The gate to our college was barred, and I hammered on the guardhouse window. The guard grumbled but let me back in. Our building was also chained; after ten minutes of my ringing the bell, the night porter emerged in his undershirt and boxer shorts to open up the foreigners' dormitory, lock me inside it, then rechain the handles. I had remembered my key and slipped into our apartment. A breeze brushed against my cheeks—Mary had left both balcony doors open—and the living room curtains were suddenly pregnant with a spring wind.

"Zhou?" I said without thinking.

6

WATERMELONS

In June, Beijing was overrun with watermelons. Every free-market stall and government stand—whether vendors of vegetables, meats or bean curd, whether trading from a truck, roadside table or alley doorway—all suddenly sold melons. The invasion, launched in late May, was equaled in intensity only by the city's fabled October cabbages. But the cabbage, though simple and trustworthy, paled next to its spring rival. Melons were sensually spherical; cabbages were functionally cylindrical. Melons bore the lush tones of Asian jungles, cabbages the sallow pigments of stagnant ponds. Melons begged artistry in their displays: Khmer temples, Zen rock gardens. Cabbages were pitched from the back of a truck, piled haphazardly, forgotten. No one who had eaten a melon, especially as Beijingers ate them—tearing the fruit apart bare-handed, then plunging their faces into the moist center—could deny the bacchanalian overtones. And the cabbage? A staple of winter dining, the cabbage was stored for months on a windowsill or back porch, to be brought indoors to thaw only when a trip to the market yielded nothing but gnarled potatos or more cabbages. The vegetable had no smell, except rot, and no texture; it looked like wallpaper and tasted like cardboard. The odor of boiling cabbage was disheartening, and diners squeezed a limp leaf between their chopsticks, shook off the water, stuffed it into the their mouths, chewed and swallowed, with scant pleasure. For a people obsessed with freshness in cuisine, the cabbage was an onerous duty performed, in part, to survive until the melon days of May and June.

What sweet days they were! The hunt commenced with a thirst, a tingle, casual eye contact with a stand that featured a split melon and a chalkboard listing a price per *jin*.*

The price was constantly in flux, and astute vendors boasted their discounts by leaving the old figure on display, slashed from 1.3 in the morning to 1.1 at noon to an even *yuan* after siesta. The sale was slow and purposeful. First, the shopper posed questions: were the melons ripe? Was the flesh pink through and through, were the juices sweet as honey? Next, a fruit was chosen from the pile and squeezed, shaken, sniffed and, most important, listened to. The customer hoisted the globe to his ear and went *ping!* with the finger and thumb of his free hand. Listening for what? People explained with difficulty: for a sound, almost a musical tone, that was extremely particular, extremely exact, impossible to pinpoint. (Mary and I never found it. We stood, watermelons raised like shot puts, ears pressed to the cool skin and heard absolutely nothing.) If the *ping!* was inconclusive, the shopper rejected the specimen, or else requested a viewing of its guts. The vendor plunged a knife partway into the fruit, carved out a pyramid and removed the wedge for inspection. The client could only look and sniff. When he was satisfied, the wedge was reinserted and the melon was weighed. In the evening, with the prospect of fresh truckloads of the fruit at dawn, offers plummeted to 80 and 60 and to as low as 40 *fen* a *jin*. Bargaining could turn ugly, fueled by rumors that merchants carried out nocturnal slaughters of unsold shipments, carcasses tossed into ditches to prevent prices from further collapsing. The season lasted barely a month, and the passion for watermelons was extreme, making for a volatile market. People ate melons three and four times a

*A unit of measure, equal to approximately half a kilogram.

day, ate them with meals, between meals, *as* meals, for snacks at work, for snacks on the road. People smeared themselves with the fruit in public, slurped and burbled, spat seeds, heaved canoe-shaped rinds over balconies and into gardens. By early June, melon mania was in full swing, and a bumper crop had resulted in not only lower prices but taller displays, larger temples, more contemplative rock gardens.

What was it about watermelons? Apples, oranges, finger bananas from Hainan island: no other fruit (never mind lowly vegetables) could compete. Melons addressed something fundamental in Bei-jingers: an oral fixation, perhaps, but even more simply a desire to seek pleasure in the fleeting moment. The watermelon tasted best eaten right away. Often it *had* to be consumed quickly, voraciously, without regard for consequences. Quick to ripen, quicker to spoil, melons were desperate fruit, and often ended up on the plates of people who were themselves frazzled. Eat me, the fruit begged. Eat me now!

Dinner on the evening of June 3 was supposed to feature local cui-sine prepared by Zhang Naiying. But Naiying, recently returned from another bout of tour-guiding, had meetings all day with university departments and political parties she was nominally a member of, nominally implicated in, and from which she had so far failed to extri-cate herself. Rather than reschedule the meal, Mary and I agreed to cook, and caved in to pressure from Shu Sheyu to prepare his favorite Western delicacy, fried chicken. In the kitchen, we kept cool by chomping on refrigeratered watermelons, bought in the morning for one *yuan* a *jin*.

As usual, Zhao Zhenkai arrived fifteen minutes early. "I didn't want to be late," he explained. Zhao presented a gift: a melon. "I bargained with the peddler," he said proudly. "Eighty *fen* a *jin*."

Naiying waited five minutes to appear—she was determined to quash rumors of a romance between her and Zhao—and also lugged an offering up three flights. "Prices were excellent this afternoon," Naiying said, rolling the globe onto the counter. "Sixty *fen* per *jin*, and the man gave me an extra *jin* free because of my smile!" Zhao's face fell.

Another knock on the door had us all glancing at the two watermel-ons already in the queue. Happily, Shu Sheyu entered the apartment accompanied by neither a piece of fruit nor, unfortunately, the jazz lover Sun Zhimo, who claimed he was sick but was actually, Shu explained, "just depressed about tomorrow." Everyone accepted the explanation without comment. Substituting for Sun Zhimo was a member of Shu's entourage, a sophomore from Henan province who answered only to her English name. The girl's dedication to foreign language learning was admirable, but the name was not: Nixon. "Chosen in honor of the American president," the student explained to Zhao Zhenkai, who had never met her.

"You mean Richard Nixon?"

"His visit to our country inspired the current policy of openness," Nixon said.

"But what about Watergate?" Zhao said.

Small and frumpy, with buck teeth and a smile that wrinkled her nose, Nixon looked harmless. She was not. "All politicians are corrupt," she answered brightly. "We cannot judge them like normal human beings."

Shu clapped with glee.

"Did you teach her that?" I asked.

"Nixon is my best student," he admitted.

But Nixon had not come empty-handed. Quite the opposite: her gift was a two-hander—round, green, weighing more than a kilogram. I received the offering like a father allowed to hold his baby for the first time.

"That was very kind of you, Nixon," I said.

"How much did you pay?" Naiying asked, switching languages.

"One *yuan*," Nixon answered.

Poor kid.

"So expensive," Naiying commiserated.

"One *yuan* for the *whole* watermelon," Shu said, sensing our smugness. "Maybe twenty *fen* per *jin*."

"I haggled like an old woman!" Nixon exclaimed.

Zhao's face, not yet recovered from the first blow, dropped again. "The living room is cooler," I said, moving people from the hallway.

Mary asked Naiying about her day.

189

"Not so good," Zhang Naiying replied. Then, seeking precision, "Perhaps very bad."

"Naiying gave a presentation at the Party meeting this morning," Zhao offered maliciously.

"Presentation on what?" Mary wondered.

"The topic was 'Why Socialism Will Defeat Capitalism in the Next Century,'" she answered without a blink.

"Wow," I said.

"I would give a very short presentation," Shu said. "Two words only: 'It Won't.'"

"This presentatation would not be acceptable," Naiying explained. "Each speech has to be ten minutes, without the use of graphs or drawings. Shu's response would need to be expanded."

"'Socialism Won't Defeat Capitalism in the Next Century,'" Shu expanded. "There—eight words now."

"What did you say, Naiying?" Mary asked.

"I struggled for many hours last night, copying out newspaper articles. At the meeting this morning I recited these articles from beginning to end. It filled the time," she concluded in her resolutely neutral voice. Naiying was sometimes impossible to read: self-deprecating, sensitive to propriety, but also mischievous and quick witted. A twinkle in her eyes was often the only clue.

"Did other Party members know your answer was copied?" I asked her.

"Everyone copies answers. Sometimes we are provided sheets of information, if the topic is difficult." Naiying sipped her soda. "It was unfair of the leaders to make me comment on socialism and capitalism," she said. "Usually they ask people who have been abroad to give that presentation. These members have experiences, and can talk for hours about America. But I have no experiences, and so must rely on my imagination, and also copy."

"Do Party members criticize the West?"

"They are very critical of America. Everyone in America is a bourgeois capitalist who exploits the working class. Almost everyone in America lives in a ghetto."

190

"Sounds like a terrible place," I said.

"We think so," Naiying agreed. "Party members who criticize the West the loudest have often been to America on many occasions, in order to increase their knowledge. Most of them are awaiting visas to make further study."

"A lifelong project," Zhao said.

"But I am not complaining," Naiying said. "Others are more unfortunate than me."

Bitterness was in the air. Except for Nixon, all our guests were in the process of applying to universities in the West. Mary and I were aware of their various schemes—we had helped fill in school and visa forms, walking them into our respective embassies, past lineups of nationals outside the gates. But we also understood that, to varying degrees, our friends were not fully cognizant of each other's activities. Zhao Zhenkai knew, for example, that Naiying had applied to two American colleges, but had she told him about the possible scholarship from the University of Victoria? Likewise, while Shu Sheyu's Denmark scam was public knowledge, no one, outside ourselves, appreciated the true extent of Shu's *guanxi* with his banker friend, whose sister was engaged to the consular officer at the Danish embassy who would be reviewing Shu's case. Zhao Zhenkai had already been rejected twice by the British with the explanation that his excellent English, compounded by his sex, age and marital status, made him a probable refugee claimant. Though Zhao's encounters with officials had been reported at an earlier dinner, he had refrained, as far as we knew, from showing anyone but us the letters of support written on his behalf by members of the British Parliament, collected by the woman who was acting as Zhao's sponsor. Woven together, the threads of half-truths and partial admissions made a single fabric, and Mary and I treated it gingerly, lest a verbal stumble, a confusion over what information was classified to whom, should unravel the stitching.

The eyes of our friends were underscored with insomnia and their smiles were perpetually attentuated. Even with one another they were on guard, not suspicious so much as instinctively cautious, dizzy from tales of betrayals and dreams squelched by vengeful superiors once the details became grist for the rumor mill. The isolation must have been devastating. Tomorrow a friend might pack his bags and slip away; a day later a colleague could turn up after years as a phantom and reclaim her job and apartment. Doors were slamming, especially in the formal exchange programs with American universities, whose administrators were wearying of inviting a teacher for a year only to have to deal with the scholar's decision afterward to seek asylum. Waiting lists for the exchanges stretched into the next century, yet each departing academic was possibly the last of a breed, the last to "get out" before the program was canceled. Solo fliers fared no better: embassies in Beijing were politely, or impolitely, telling visa applicants to go home. Anyone single, under forty and blessed with foreign language skills was deemed an unacceptable risk. Even so, thousands of people were queuing up outside embassies for days and nights, in sunshine and rain, under the intimidating stares of soldiers, the glare of plainclothes police, the scrutiny of informants planted in crowds, in order to become forlorn, homesick refugees whose new lives would be forever cast in the melancholy hues of exile.

Since January, a stream of fresh regulations had succeeded in tripling the number of hoops the applicant had to jump through in order even to make it to Beijing Capital Airport. They included a buy-out clause, equal to the amount the state had contributed toward an undergraduate degree, for any teacher who quit his or her teaching post before a minimum five-year sentence had been served. Starting again in mid-May, those staying in Beijing had to endure daily meetings with departments, political affairs mandarins, administration officials, public security representatives and the Party itself, wherein a threat regarding any observation of the anniversary of the Turmoil was conveyed with the subtlety of a gun barrel pressed to the temple.

"Was the English department meeting better?" I asked Naiying.

But first we had to pause to bear witness to Shu's decapitation of a beer bottle. Hoping to impress Nixon, Shu forswore safety measures and instead stood the bottle on the coffee table and simply rammed his face into it, like a man impaling himself on a knife. The cap stayed on, the bottle toppled over, and Shu came up grinning, bleeding in the gums and lower lip.

"Jesus, Shu," I said.

"Something must be wrong with that beer," he said, checking for loose teeth.

"You are bloody, Mr. Shu," a pale Nixon offered.

"I don't mind," he replied.

Mary rapped Shu on the arm with a bottle opener. His huge face was suddenly a mask: mocking, evil, mouth made up to suggest a carnivor fresh from a kill. Shu accepted the opener, smiling defiantly.

"You can use a towel in the bathroom," Mary hinted.

"What for?"

She turned to Naiying. "Did Dean Shen mention the anniversary during the meeting?" she asked.

"I think so."

"Were you there?"

"For three hours," she confirmed. "Most of the time I read magazines or whispered with friends I had not seen in many months. Also I slept a little."

"A *lot*," Zhao corrected. "I sat next to Naiying. She slept longer than any other teacher at the meeting. Maybe an hour, without waking up once."

"Zhao!"

"Dean Shen informed us to be wary of the teachings of Fang Lizhi," Zhao said, rolling his glass between his palms. "He explained the details of Fang's dangerous thinking about democracy and human rights, so we would be familiar with them."

"Do you remember this?" I asked Naiying.

"I was awake for the interesting speeches," she explained. "Dean Shen has excellent knowledge of Fang Lizhi's ideas, and denounced them very well. Most of what he said had been copied from the *People's Daily*, but the dean added many of his own thoughts. He also read out a bulletin from the government that named Wang Juntao and Chen Ziming as the Black Hands behind the Turmoil. We were pleased to receive this information."

Wang Juntao and Chen Ziming were older dissidents whose experiences with Wei Jingsheng and the Democracy Wall movement had earned them the title "professional revolutionaries" and several years' imprisonment. Wang and Chen played quiet but active roles in 1989, advising young leaders like Wang Dan, and they were eventually hunted down and arrested. Neither had been heard from since. The government's penchant for using Party and work-unit meetings to familiarize the masses with its enemies was legendary. Many intellectuals first became acquainted with Fang Lizhi in the mid-1980s, thanks to packets of his writings that the Party disseminated among the ranks, with instructions that the documents be studied carefully for rejection and ridicule. In the absence of a free press, such pipelines were vital, and if the irony escaped those handing out the information, it was certainly not lost on citizens benefiting from these ludicrous propaganda exercises.

"So when did you fall asleep?" I asked.

"Shortly afterward," Naiying replied, "when the political commissar began to give out instructions on how intellectuals should respond to the anniversary of the Turmoil."

We all waited. Only Zhao Zhenkai could fill us in. "Don't look at me!" he laughed.

"Were you also asleep?"

"I was reading an old *Time* magazine," Zhao said, easing into a smile. "An article about Donald Trump's marriage. His girlfriend is very beautiful, but his wife is very angry."

"Was there anything on Beijing in the issue?" I asked.

"I am not so interested in those things," Zhao said straight-faced. "Politics is boring,"

"Everything is boring!" Nixon piped in.

"Can we eat now?" Shu said.

"You must have heard a little of what the political officer said ...?" I pressed.

"He spoke for one hour," Zhao answered reluctantly. "But said nothing. It would not be in his best interest to either speak for less than one hour or to say anything. Therefore, he said nothing, nothing, nothing, about tomorrow."

"This is the message," Naiying agreed.

"What about the history department, Shu?"

"The chicken smells delicious ..." he offered.

"What did they say at your meeting?"

"Nothing."

"What about tomorrow?"

"Nothing!"

"I'll get the food," Mary said.

During the interval, Nixon serenaded us with song. Her voice lacked strength, but for a nineteen-year-old in a room full of teachers, she was remarkably composed.

"Wo yao gei ni wo de zui qiu,
Hai you wo de ziyou,
Ke ni que zong shi xiao wo
Yi wu shuo you"

("I want to give you my hopes,
And also my freedom,
But all you do is laugh,
And tell me I am nothing")

"Very nice," I said.

Shu frowned. "That is my song," he protested.

Next the girl examined the calligraphy. She stood before the sheet with her hands sunk into her pockets, bouncing from foot to foot and humming Cui Jian. The rice paper was badly faded and cross-apartment drafts had frayed the corners.

"What's this funny stuff?" she wondered.

"We don't know," Zhao answered on our behalf. "No one can decide if the calligraphy is very old or very new and very beautiful or very ugly."

"It's a testament to our traditional culture," Naiying said, eyes twinkling.

Shu disagreed. He had gone into the kitchen to "help" Mary and me serve the meal but had actually only swiped a piece of chicken, sniffed the other dishes, then wandered back into the living room.

Now he sidled up to Nixon and, using a drumstick as pointer, began to read the first column of ideographs. He stumbled almost immediately, changed his mind twice, complained that the writing was sloppy, and finally decided the calligraphy was a poem on an unclear subject composed during an unspecified dynasty in the misty past.

"What do *you* think the calligraphy means, Nixon?" I asked.

Nixon wrinkled her nose. "Who cares?" she replied.

"Good answer," Zhao said.

Only two guests were showing any appetite. Shu Sheyu had stripped four pieces of chicken in five minutes. Asked his opinion of the bird, he shrugged. "Tastes like blood," he said, displaying his gums. Nixon loaded her plate with bean salad, lettuce salad, bread and cheese, but then whispered to Mary that, as far as she could tell, we had forgotten to *cook* half the dishes. Mary apologized for our absentmindedness, encouraging the undergraduate to concentrate on the chicken.

"Your ancestors in Henan province ate fried chicken," I said to her, referring to Shu's boast that Western claims to the dish were shallow and self-deceiving.

"How do you know this?" Nixon asked.

"During the Tang dynasty," I continued, determined to liven up the conversation. "Or maybe the Ming. Right, Shu?"

"I don't know what you are talking about," Shu said.

Nixon took matters into her own hands. "My ancestors are all in the cemetery," she said. "Who cares what foods they ate? I care only about today, and tomorrow. So everybody cheer up!"

"Tomorrow will not be so cheery," Zhao said.

"Day after tomorrow, then," she amended.

"Things will be better on June 5?"

"Sure! Much better," Nixon said, sounding like a self-help guru. "You wait and see, Mr. Zhao."

Mr. Zhao agreed to wait and see. Mr. Shu interrupted his gorging to defend his effervescent pupil. "Nixon is an optimist," he said.

"Nixon is full of beans," Zhao added, cracking a smile.

"The beans are not cooked," Nixon said, shaking her head. "I cannot eat them."

At nine o'clock Shu rose and, after turning off the overhead light, put on the television. The screen glowed to life. "Special progam tonight," he announced.

"About the Turmoil?" I said foolishly.

"A famous movie," Naiying said. *"The Burning of the Summer Palace*, starring Liu Xiaoqing as the Empress Dowager Cixi. The movie is shown this evening to prove that foreigners were responsible for the student movement."

"Also to take advantage of our national character," Zhao said, picking up a *Herald-Tribune* from the desk. "Make our blood boil at the injustices committed by outsiders, instead of those done by the PLA."

"This movie is boring!" Nixon said, rocking up and down on the couch.

"Quiet," Shu commanded.

The Burning of the Summer Palace told the story of the sacking of the imperial palace in 1860 by British forces under the command of Lord Elgin, former governor general of Canada. The invasion was a repulsive act of imperialism and constituted the first of many Western assaults upon the previously sacroscant, and impenetrable, capital city. The British were able to waltz into Beijing, march across it and then pillage and burn the summer residence of the emperor Qianlong owing, in large part, to the blundering of the Qing government. Given that official history had declared the Qing emperors despots whose destructive feudal mind-set cleared the ground for the proletariat revolution, the film would not have been expected to flatter either side in the dispute. Indeed, in casting parts, producers managed to round up the most mottled, goitrous-eyed bunch of Westerners imaginable to play the British. They looked, one and all, like a gang of bikers in pith helmets, and even *we* found them alien and repulsive. Members of the Qing court, the majority of whom responded to the crisis by fleeing Beijing, were portrayed, in contrast, as doddering but decent, while Cixi herself, a woman of dubious character, came across as cagey and intelligent. *The Burning of the Summer Palace* climaxed with the bikers rampaging through the imperial playground while the government slinked off to Manchuria, leaving behind negotiators to sign away even more of the country to foreigners.

The film was certainly entertaining. It also featured English subtitles, an aberration that Mary and I thought astonishing, but guests shrugged off.

"Why would the movie need subtitles?" I said. "Isn't it just for local consumption?"

"Shh," Shu said.

"Perhaps the only copy available had English titles," Naiying suggested.

Zhao looked up from his newspaper. "The subtitles are a warning," he said.

Nixon, Mary and I cleared the table. In the kitchen, Shu's student repeated her conviction that the movie was boring, that, in fact, everything was boring, then outlined without a trace of false modesty her plan to use her father's *guanxi* to obtain a visa to study in the United States during her final undergraduate year, thereby skirting the regulations that would block her escape after graduation. Grinning, Nixon added a footnote: once out the door, she would not be back, ever. We believed her.

"The watermelons look tasty," she said. "Especially mine!"

We marched into the living room with the three melons and plunked them down, along with a knife. Shu glanced over, fingered each globe, hoisted two of them to his ear, made a *ping!*, all the while keeping his eyes on the TV screen. Then he seized the knife and split the chosen fruit, the blade slicing through pulp and skin to the wooden surface below. Next he grasped a half, tore it into quarters, stuffed a wedge into his face and commenced slurping. Remarkably, Shu's gaze never strayed from *The Burning of the Summer Palace*, even with watermelon bobbing before his eyes. Other people also tucked into the dessert, though not as violently.

"How many times have you seen this movie?" I asked Shu.

"Huh?"

"How many times—?"

"Maybe ten times."

"Naiying?"

"Perhaps seven times."

"Zhao?"

Zhao tried wrenching a half melon apart with his hands, à la Shu. His forearms trembled; the fruit emitted faint sucking sounds, but still would not be divided. "I've gotten watermelon juice on the *Herald-Tribune*," he apologized.

The table was now a marsh of seed and sweet water, with rinds upright in the pool. "It's okay," I said.

"I have seen it three or four times," Zhao replied. "But never as a propaganda film. This is a new angle."

"Who is it a warning to?" I asked.

"You," Zhao said simply.

"Me?"

"We the people are united," he smiled.

"United against—?"

"Whatever we are told to be united against."

"Told by movies?"

He shrugged. Shu, however, had a comment. "Everybody keep quiet," he said.

"Everybody cheer up!" Nixon added.

Nobody cheered up. Instead we ate watermelon and watched the final hour of the film. By the end of *The Burning of the Summer Palace*, all our guests were absorbed by the movie's jingoism and lost in melancholy, and the night fizzled out shortly afterward.

"Next party I will invite my classmates," Nixon said. "Then it will not be so boring!"

At the door, I brown-bagged a selection of newspapers and magazines for Zhao—it was unwise to be seen leaving the foreigners' dormitory with materials—and assured him there was no rush to return them. I also took Shu aside to remind him yet again of his promise to share his theory about why the country was in such a state. Shu looked at me through glassy eyes. "Soon," he said sullenly.

Naiying heard us. "Shu is drunk," she explained, touching his hand. Naiying apologized once more for being unable to prepare the meal.

"Next time," Mary said, taking her friend's arm.

We went down to Tiananmen Square the following afternoon. The day was sun drenched and breezy, a clear sky promising no dust storms or sudden squalls. Rumors of a midnight fracas at Beida and a dawn patrol of our campus by soldiers disguised as local police seemed to be confirmed by the empty city streets and deserted shopping districts. After managing seats on three successive buses—first such luck in two years—we walked past the Beijing Hotel to the Forbidden City. There we followed a sidewalk shaded by a red-brick wall. Eventually the wall turned ninety-degrees shortly before meeting a ceremonial creek, spanned by five marble rainbow bridges and fronted by two columns. Atop the columns were winged sentinels called *hou*, with stone lions positioned before them to guard the Gate of Heavenly Peace, the first of four towers leading into the royal palace and the rostrum from which imperial edicts were once issued.

On reaching Mao Zedong's portrait, hung over the middle of five gateways, we stopped and faced south. All time in the country was determined by the time at this spot, and all distances were judged by their remoteness from this patch of concrete. The concrete protected hallowed ground, and to tread upon it was to sense the tremors of continuous history and culture. Standing outside the palace, dwarfed by imperial guard towers and Stalinist edifices, dazzled by the glories of vanished dynasties and the baggage of current ones, a person could only be humbled, wobbly legged in the face of such splendor.

Across Chang'an Avenue, happily, was the official people's sanctuary. Once an elegant city square, Tiananmen had been enlarged shortly after Liberation to provide the masses with a place of their own adjacent to the Forbidden City. So vast and welcoming was the new Tiananmen that it was also selected as the site for Chairman Mao's mausoleum. His embalmed corpse lay snug in an airport hangar that consumed the bottom third of the square. Actually, if Mao was comfortable on Tiananmen, he was likely the only one. There were no trees, no flower beds, and the only greenery—locked behind a fence—embowered the mausoleum. And rest areas? The base of the Monument to the People's Heroes has steps, but a guard was stationed there to shoo away the weary. (The obelisk had been closed to the public since the Turmoil.) Visitors who wished to relax, drink a soda (vendors were barred), or watch kites flirt above the cityscape had little choice but to hunker down on pavement. Few bothered. The square broiled in summer, froze in winter, and even the faintest wind, frustrated by urban obstacles, exploded onto Tiananmen with the glee of a bulldog released from a pen. A person eager for a stroll could anticipate sweating, shivering, getting soaked in a downpour or staggered by a gust. If the stroll was at an odd hour of the day, in the wake of a disturbance, on an anniversary or on certain traditional festivals, or if the stroller were spotted acting inappropriately (consorting with undesirables, chatting with a foreigner, even loitering with an other-than-blank expression on the face) then, in addition to the physical and psychological discomfort of Tiananmen's layout, the individual could look forward to being accosted by plainclothes police, hustled to the curb, shoved into a van.

Today, though, Beijingers were spared such discomforts; the square was sealed off by a flimsy chain of soldiers. Squads of unarmed teenagers in uniforms that flapped in the breeze and the same black slippers worn by their grandmothers, because the fabric soothed their bound feet, marched around and around Tiananmen's rim and passed back and forth through the underground walkways. Given the paltry numbers of onlookers who hung about the fringes, the services of *real* infantry—that is, men prepared to kill—would obviously not be required. Surrounding us in front of the Gate of Heavenly Peace, already surveyed by cameras mounted on street lamps, were dozens of Public Security Bureau agents, soldiers, Westerners and a few brave locals. An old man wore a black armband. A young woman slipped on a white bandana, approached the curb as if to cross Chang'an, then hastily removed the cloth and walked away. A middle-aged couple squatted on one of the bridges, weeping. Questioned by three secret police, they quietly departed. Two Asian-Americans swaggered about the gateway snapping photos of each other at stiff attention beneath the picture of Mao.

We lasted an hour in the heat. What was there to wait for? Even if Tiananmen were suddenly to be opened, cleared of army, police, loudspeakers and rooftop surveillance systems, and even if citizens were invited back onto it, invited to admire the fenced-in garden, stretch out on the nonexistent benches, doze in the shade of imaginary trees, offered a heartfelt apology, an explanation, shown records of what happened, who died, who killed them, and even if senior government leaders personally laid commemorative wreaths for the massacred, ordered memorials carved into the concrete, flowers strewn over chalk marks, and promised on the Bible or *The Communist Manifesto* or even Confucius's *Analects* that it would never happen again—even then, the square would remain a desolate place. Like the Forbidden City, like the grotesque buildings surrounding the site, Tiananmen was a rectangular hole in the heart of Beijing, something best driven around, best forgotten.

In the evening, I climbed the six flights to Shu Sheyu's room to ask if he wanted company for his final commemorative turn of the track. Shu's door was locked, a white carnation stuffed into his message envelope. I tried Guo Yidong's room across the hallway, also without success. But I met up with Guo who was, of course, already down on the field. He shook my hand warmly.

"I would, ahem, enjoy a conversation this evening," he said.

"Are you okay?"

"Fine, except for a mild cold."

"No metaphysical balance yet, Guo?"

"Perhaps not," he confessed, adjusting his glasses. "Perhaps I am destined to fluctuate permanently between *yin* and *yang*, to, let me see, oscil—, oscil—"

I provided the verb.

"Nice word," he said. "To oscillate between the two."

"Does that bother you?"

"It is distressing. My *chi* refuses to flow smoothly and I am unable to work things through my mind, expel them and be free once again. I remain trapped by illusions. According to one way of thinking, this represents a, ahem, a ..." Guo hiccuped, pushed his glasses back up his nose.

"Wait a second," I said, staring at his ancient, thick-lensed spectacles for the first time in a year.

"... personal failure," he said, completing the sentence.

"When—?" I asked.

"A week ago," Guo answered. "There is too much dust in the air here."

"Is that why—?"

"Only partially," he interrupted. His manner was strangely forceful tonight. With anyone else I would have read anger and frustration in the voice. But Guo Yidong? "I resumed wearing glasses in part because I was, let me see, unable to strengthen my eyes through Taoist exercises. More practically, I wanted to study books."

I nodded.

"I acted," Guo explained.

"Thereby finding meaning?"

"Not so far," he admitted. "But that should not be the point. Reading books is the point. Studying more intensively, more, could I say, directedly, about traditional medicine and philosophy—these are, for me, meanings."

"But externals?" I asked.

"Perhaps."

"And therefore illusory?"

He hiccuped, clasped then unclasped his hands, repositioned the glasses one more time. Sensing his distress—his thinking was an apostasy for a Taoist—I insisted on a quiet lap. The pause allowed me to concentrate on a bizarre activity going on within our loop. Though the track was still and the basketball courts were vacant, at midfield there stood a coven of witches sporting the telltale yellow armbands. Unless my own eyes deceived me, the *lianhefangwei*, each and every one in her sixties or better, were tossing around a grapefruit.

"What in the world ...?" I said.

Guo looked up. "Ah, yes," he said blandly. "It is the fashion these days."

"What do you call it?"

"Baseball."

The women had no catching mitts, which was fine: their throws bounced, occasionally arced upward, but mostly rolled over the field like lawn bowls. Each toss elicited cackles from the athletes. One vigorous effort sent the softball toward us. I picked it up.

"Those ladies are spies, Guo," I said, squeezing the ball between my hands.

"Neighborhood watch," he corrected.

"Tonight of all nights, you'd think they'd be busy peeking into apartment windows and informing on students who left the campus."

"Perhaps they are taking a coffee break," he said, grinning at the colloquial expression.

A spy-on-her-coffee-break called for the baseball. I offered it to Guo, but he declined. Left-handed, my toss was a lob that soared higher and higher into the twilight sky and veered farther and farther off course. When the softball finally landed, it was forty meters from the nearest grandmother. I shouted an apology. The *lianhefangwei* applauded my skill.

"Interesting," Guo said.

I rubbed my arm.

"Could I ask you a question, Charlie?"

"Please."

"From your perspective as a foreigner and a friend, how do you see the situation here?"

The question was starkly out of character. Still, I took it seriously.

"Mary and I went to the Lama Temple last week," I said, referring to a Buddhist temple in northeast Beijing. "We spent most of the morning admiring the statue at the rear of the complex." Located in the Tower of Infinite Happiness, the temple was a three-story wooden structure constructed *around* the largest indoor Buddha in the world. The statue measured twenty-six meters in height, with eight meters actually planted into the ground. It had been carved from a single trunk of sandlewood and transported to Beijing from Lhasa in 1783, a gift of the seventh Dalai Lama. "Do you know the figure?" I wondered.

"Maitreya," Guo answered. "The Buddha to Come."

"The statue is beautiful," I continued, "but too tall for such a narrow building. It's impossible to gain a perspective on the Buddha. I can only ever see his feet and knees. Up to the waist, maximum."

"Even with your glasses?"

"I get dizzy craning my neck," I said, acknowledging Guo's attempt at humor, also out of character. "And the lighting in the hall is poor. There we were, before a great work of art, with the guidebook explaining about Maitreya's headdress and intricately carved jewelry, the hundreds of additional paintings of the Buddha on the walls and ceiling around the statue, and all I could see were the feet!"

"Interesting," Guo repeated, his brow furrowed.

"*That's* my perspective on the situation here," I hastened to add.

"The feet?"

"And the knees. To the waist, maximum ..." He was staring at me.

"It's an analogy, Guo," I said. "Your philosophers use them all the time."

"I did not mean the national situation," he said, smiling at my dimness. "According to traditional thinking, that is irrelevant: each individual should look after his or her own, let me see, needs. I meant *my* situation. How do you view it?"

"Your situation?"

"My, ahem, my, could I say, life?"

I stopped. Guo kicked at the pebbles on the track. His slippers had worn through, exposing both big toes, and his track pants—the same pants used in winter, minus the underclothes—were threadbare.

"Well," I said. "I think, I mean, if I was in your ... Are you really asking?"

"It is of growing interest to me," he said.

"What is?"

"My life."

"Okay," I said. "From my perspective, you should try again to arrange a transfer to the college of traditional medicine. You should send letters, make calls, give Dean Shen gifts, give the deans and administrators at the other school gifts—*anything* to make it happen."

He hiccuped. "Because ...?"

"People need to be fulfilled," I said. "They need to feel good about what they do, how they live."

"Aah."

"I know it's selfish," I said, "vain and self-deceiving. I know we are imprisoned by our desires. But ..."

"Yes?"

Lacking the wisdom to continue, I shrugged. Guo accepted my limitation, and we walked in comfortable silence. It was nine o'clock in the evening on June 4, 1990, and Guo and I were on a field in the center of a campus where five thousand people lived on the outskirts of a city of ten million, and it was like standing alone on the edge of a desert, gaze fixed on a vanishing point of sand, a dissolving sky, and struggling to *feel* something—sadness, regret, fury—but only managing emptiness.

"What about you?" Guo finally said.

"Me?"

"Did you find a, ahem, shape to all this?"

"You remembered."

"Of course," he said simply.

"Maybe," I replied.

"Then you are fulfilled?"

"It's a *terrible* shape, Guo," I whispered, stricken with shame.

"You ask too much."

"I know."

"Westerners often—"

"I know. I'm sorry."

We reached the section of the track nearest the gate. I broke off to be with Mary. Guo Yidong wished me goodnight. How much longer would he circle the field? Awhile longer, Guo answered. Until he had worked things through his mind, expelled them, and was free once again.

EPILOGUE

Two weeks after the first anniversary of the Tiananmen massacre, I flew from Beijing to Tibet, in part to better appreciate Zhou Shuren's dream. Unable to obtain a visa for regions outside Lhasa, I wandered the capital for five dreadful days, appalled by the grandeur of a celestial city where terrible things were occurring within, it seemed, God's own reach. The government in Beijing is engaged in a slow and brutal domestication of the Tibetan people. Tibet constitutes almost one-quarter of China's empire, and the mathematics are straightforward: east of the massive Tibetan plateau are more than a billion human beings, while within the current borders of the Tibetan Autonomous Region lingers a scant, and dwindling, population of four million, proprietors of too much land, too much natural bounty and a way of life too helpless, isolated and easily targeted. Compound these demographics with the rapacious hunger of the Chinese government for fresh natural resources to plunder, a virgin environment to violate, wildlife to slaughter, windswept plains wherein to develop and test nuclear weapons and a bully's compulsion to keep reasserting his superiority, and the situation in Tibet can be seen to be desperate. How could young Beijing intellectuals like Zhou Shuren possibly conceive of this tragic place as an escape? How could I ever have conjured an idyll of mountains and skies without accounting for half a million PLA troops, labor camps stocked with Tibetan and Chinese dissidents, nuclear launch sites, valleys stripped of their trees and hills robbed of their minerals? There may be no Shangri-la in Tibet or anywhere else, but the desire for one is eternal; and for most people, desire, I now understand, is everything.

Mary and I left Beijing again at the end of July. Our departure this time around was better: leisurely goodbyes, last visits to favorite spots, modest epiphanies. While packing, we debated what to do with the sheet of calligraphy that still clung to the living room wall. The man who had sent it to us—a French student we knew in 1988—solved the problem by showing up on campus. He confessed to authorship; the calligraphy was indeed the work of a clumsy foreigner. Were our Chinese friends, except Li Feigan, merely being polite? Having us on? We kept the sheet as a reminder.

The trials of Tiananmen activists began in January 1991, under the media cover of the Persian Gulf War. Held in secret, without a jury, the trials were crude and perfunctory: the counterrevolutionary appeared, received his or her sentence, then disappeared into the gulag. In many cases, these brief court appearances were the first indication, twelve to eighteen months after the fact, that these people had been in police custody.

Wang Dan was given a relatively light four-year term, the result, according to officials, of his having both confessed his crimes and informed on others. Guo Haifeng, one of the students who knelt on the steps of the Great Hall of the People to entreat the leadership to accept a petition, also received four years, with dozens more scholars meriting lesser sentences. The harshest punishments were reserved for the fabled Black Hands who had, according to authorities, "formed a conspiracy to manipulate the students on the square." These hardened dissidents absorbed the brunt of the Party's wrath. Veteran human-rights activist Ren Wanding, one of the few who refused to recant, was given seven years. Professional revolutionaries Chen Ziming and Wang Juntao, accused of plotting to overthrow the government, earned thirteen-year punishments for their repeat offenses. Others, including several workers, were tried in total secrecy, and either executed (as dozens of workers were immediately after the crackdown) or sentenced to even longer terms. Wei Jingsheng, of course, continues to languish in a prison somewhere, presuming he is still alive.

On June 4, 1991, Mary and I made a more personal tally. Friends had fared better than we'd dared hope. Shu Sheyu remained at the college, apparently close to finalizing the details of his Danish adventure, as did Guo Yidong, who was still ruminating over whether to reapply to study traditional medicine. Zhao Zhenkai quit teaching to work for an international bank, and also relinquished his vague designs on Zhang Naiying in favor of a woman at the office. Naiying, her divorce from both the institute and the Party complete, was busy filling out scholarship applications and escorting Taiwanese nationals around the tourist sites. Li Feigan's dinner at the Beijing Hotel paid off; the old man he buttered up landed him a job as a sales representative with a government trading company. Intensive politicking also secured Li a residency card and a room on campus. Yu Wei found a government position as well. Remarkably, the student Ding Luojin carried through with her outrageous escape plan and wrote to us from the Shenzhen special economic zone in January. She was a secretary, shared an apartment with three other office staff, and was at last "out" of China. By June, however, she was back in: the job was boring, the living was arduous, and besides, she missed her family and friends. Rather than reappear at her work unit, Luojin decided to assail the Beijing market, concentrating on locating a position as an English teacher.

Bei Hua, in contrast, never left the capital. We received one letter from him, minus a return address. He was, we gathered, absent without permission from his Changchun high school, residing illegally in Beijing, ostracized, penniless, happy. To date, Zhou Shuren has also written only once, a Christmas card hinting that he had gone to Tibet, at least for a while, but then returned to the institute of his own accord. Zhou had still not been betrayed by the roommate and continued to flail about in the college safety net, thanks to Dean Shen's mysterious benevolence. The dean, who was never punished for his activism, is apparently now a radio personality.

Something crucial *didn't* happen to these people. Having survived the massacre—our college was lucky to avoid casualties—they were forced in the year following to endure incessant reminders of how bitter failure tasted and how futile hopes could be. At the same time, though, measures designed to pummel them into submission failed in the end; our friends may have been prone to bouts of moroseness and ambivalence, but they also kept on with what they had been doing before June 4, 1989. Not only that, but they persisted in attempting to piece together meaningful and dignified lives with full knowledge of the costs involved. Even if that knowledge only further convinced a Zhang Naiying or Zhou Shuren to flee China, it was knowledge, still. The Tiananmen student movement served as a lesson in the exigencies of private needs and public welfare.

And Cui Jian's blindfold? The disagreement over the singer's gesture—was it an act of defiance or ego?—had bothered me since first seeing the *Herald-Tribune* photo in Beijing. Back in Montreal I attended a screening of a British documentary on Cui, and learned that the blindfold was a prop used during a song called "A Piece of Red Cloth." The documentary featured footage of a concert Cui Jian gave in Beijing in April 1990 that Mary and I had tried unsuccessfully to attend. All the band members wore strips of red cloth, with Cui's strip blinding his eyes. I copied down a partial translation of "A Piece of Red Cloth." Cui sang:

> "The day you discovered a piece of red cloth
> To cover my eyes and block the sky
> I said that I saw happiness."

Later in the song, he offered a line that jarred me from my seat. Cui Jian sang: "I feel this is no desert." Unsure if I had read the subtitles right, I waited for him to repeat the phrase. He did.

> *"I feel this is no desert."*